Isaac Murphy

BLACK LIVES

———

Yale University Press's Black Lives series seeks to tell the fullest range of stories about the both notable and overlooked Black figures who profoundly shaped world history. Each book in our series is intended to add a chapter to our larger understanding of the breadth of the experiences of Black people as these have unfolded through time. Using a variety of approaches, the books in this series trace the indelible contributions that individuals of African descent have made to their worlds, and explore how their lives embody and shape the changing conditions of modernity and challenge definitions of race and practices of racism in their societies.

Isaac Murphy

———

THE RISE AND FALL
OF A BLACK JOCKEY

———

Katherine C. Mooney

———

Black Lives

Yale University Press | New Haven and London

The Black Lives series is supported with a gift from
the Germanacos Foundation.

Published with assistance from Jonathan W. Leone, Yale '86.

Yale University Press books may be purchased in quantity for
educational, business, or promotional use. For information,
please e-mail sales.press@yale.edu (U.S. office) or
sales@yaleup.co.uk (U.K. office).

Set in Freight Text Pro type by Integrated Publishing Solutions.
Printed in the United States of America.

Library of Congress Control Number: 2022944101
ISBN 978-0-300-25442-6 (hardcover : alk. paper)

A catalogue record for this book is available from the British Library.

This paper meets the requirements of ANSI/NISO Z39.48-1992
(Permanence of Paper).

10 9 8 7 6 5 4 3 2 1

To Kim and David

CONTENTS

———

Isaac Murphy

Introduction

THE TABLE, covered in white cloths and champagne bottles, stretched through a gap in the trees. Sweating in their suits in the August heat, the guests had traveled by private railway car from New York to a dusty glade at the Jersey shore for this party. They were the Salvator Club, and they'd come to celebrate their namesake, the stallion acclaimed as the best horse American racing had ever produced. "Salvator," pronounced the *Anaconda Standard,* "as the greatest horse in history, is exerting a distinct influence upon his time." Surely there would soon be "Salvator hats and neckties, Salvator cocktails, Salvator cigars, Salvator playing cards."[1] There were other stars in Thoroughbred racing, then among the most popular sports in the United States, but New York power brokers didn't stage elaborate outdoor banquets for other horses. They celebrated Salvator because the bigstriding bright chestnut exerted the centripetal fascination of the greatest athletes. And they respected his owner, James Ben Ali Haggin, the financier who had helped build Anaconda Copper, one of the industry-eating conglomerates that defined the Gilded Age. But they also honored his jockey, the only Black man at the table.

The Salvator Club clambake, August 1890. Isaac Murphy is seated at the round table, third from right. Keeneland Library General Collection.

His name was Isaac Murphy. You may never have heard of him. But everyone you've heard of had. He was born enslaved in 1861. His father died in the Civil War, and his mother supported him by doing domestic work. His family was one among thousands like it in the market towns of the South in the 1860s. We know his story because he didn't live in just any small town. He lived in Lexington, Kentucky, which was, in his youth, working hard to cement the place it still holds as an international center of Thoroughbred racing. Before Murphy was in his teens, he was working with horses. As an adult, he became one of the greatest jockeys in history.

When Murphy was still a child, the Thirteenth, Fourteenth, and Fifteenth Amendments to the Constitution of the United States abolished slavery and instituted birthright citizenship, due process and equal protection of the law, and the right to the franchise for Black men. In his lifetime, African Americans worked to give substance to abstractions like freedom and equality in every aspect of their lives. That was a battle through which Isaac Murphy lived and in which some of the people closest to him fought bravely. Murphy's life shows us the daily work of those people, but it also shows us the work of his employers, the men who owned the horses and also often owned the leviathans of American capital, the men who were busy building a society that elevated freedom to make money over equality before the law.

Murphy never said much in public. He may have been naturally quiet. Or he may have learned in a hard school to keep his thoughts and feelings to himself. And so people attributed to him the thoughts and feelings they wanted him to have. Telling his story is particularly challenging because he left us no personal papers and only a few interviews with reporters who may or may not have faithfully transcribed what he said. This book tries to recover the truth of his life, and part of that truth is what it must have been like to live surrounded by stories about what he meant to people and what they wanted him to be, stories that often drowned out the ones he might have told himself.

In Black communities and newspapers, celebrations of Murphy's success joined tales of other leaders in politics and the professions. In racing results and interviews, in jockeys' room photographs matter-of-factly posed alongside white colleagues, Murphy seemed to prove that a truly free and equal society was possible.

He was the example that proved the rule, the sign to point the way. But the very possibility that men like Murphy embodied sparked visceral rejection in many white Americans, who refused to live in a society where a Black man could be a successful, stylish hero. The political and legal changes that made Murphy's career possible enraged people who throughout his lifetime violently sought to reverse those changes. Meanwhile, courts and legislatures nibbled away at the new amendments to the Constitution so that their guarantees could be drained of meaning. And white Americans told their own stories to make what they were doing seem right and inevitable. They insisted that Blackness was a condition that could be described and measured and that determined a person's physical and mental capacities. These kinds of ideas about race often flourished in places assumed to be outside politics, like entertainment and sports, and they underpinned an understanding of the world in which Black people had no right to political citizenship, because they had very little right to human dignity. Successful Black people who supposedly conformed to racial hierarchy without questioning it were praised for doing so. They were the exceptions that proved the rule. And Isaac Murphy was one of the prime examples of those people. He was one of the subjects on which Americans practiced the narratives that would power the racial hierarchies that survived and reshaped themselves after slavery. The stories surrounding his life are texts that illustrate how racism has evolved in how it sorts human beings and assigns them value, how it can flex and cling and find ways to turn its inconsistencies and hypocrisies into vindications and victories.

This book seeks to depict Isaac Murphy's life from multiple angles; sometimes the narrative lingers on one particular view of him, but they are all part of his story. To tell that story is to honor the sacrifice and skill of a man who achieved feats few others have ever even approximated. To tell his story is also to tell two of the great stories of nineteenth-century America: the debates over what a world without slavery, a multiracial democracy, might look like; and the battles over who was to hold political power in an economy that increasingly resembled the corporate, wealth-polarized one we know today. And it is to recognize how similar the stories about Murphy are to those that have sprung up around generations of Black athletes over decades of civil rights struggles. His story should remind us of the stories of Joe Louis, of Jackie Robinson, of John Carlos and Tommie Smith, of Michael Jordan, of Serena Williams, of the Atlanta Dream, of Colin Kaepernick. It is on the bodies of Black athletes that we have written national accounts of citizenship and rights, of deserving and belonging.

In the last scene he wrote of his final, unfinished novel, Ralph Ellison envisioned one of his white main characters looking at a series of lithographs and suddenly seeing American history from a new perspective. He examines images of an enslaved mother, of John Brown, of Jack Johnson, and of Isaac Murphy. Maybe, he thinks, if he looks at these pictures he can grasp "the complex role played in our fractured democracy by the sports and the arts." Maybe he'll glimpse how much has been forgotten or erased, how much could have been and could still be different. Maybe he can understand something about "our fractured democracy" itself.[2]

CHAPTER 1

———

"Reputable and Entitled to Credit"

AMERICA MURPHY BURNS told the man in the pension office that there was no documentation of her son's birth. Neither she nor the boy's father could write, "and there was no means of keeping a record."[1] But she told the man some of her story, and some of the rest we can piece together.

America Murphy was born in Lexington, Kentucky, to Green and Annie Murphy, but, like many other enslaved people, she was sold or hired to a farm family in the counties that circled the town. Almost 40 percent of the people around her were enslaved, and about half of white families owned people.[2] One of those slaveholders was David Tanner of Clark County, east of Lexington; he and his wife Lydia were in their seventies and owned seven enslaved people in 1860, one of whom was probably America. On either side of them were farms belonging to other prosperous, slaveholding Tanners.[3]

About twenty miles north, in Bourbon County, was another Tanner family. America could have worked there for a time in the late 1850s, when she was in her late teens. That may be how she met Jerry Burns, an enslaved man about seven years her elder, who was legally the property of C. C. Skillman, the owner of the farm two doors down from the Bourbon County Tanners.[4] Jerry Burns was married to a woman his own age named Caroline Oliver, with whom he had three children. Mary Skillman, C. C. Skillman's wife, would later testify that they "were married as was the custom among slaves," by which she meant that they solicited permission from their owners, held a ceremony, and were afterward recognized by custom as married. Right after Christmas 1859, Jerry and America were married in the same way. In January 1861, America gave birth to a son. Two months later, so did Caroline.[5]

This account is a bare and factual one because the bare facts are all we have, and they could have many meanings—even more than the bare facts of any relationship. Marriage in slavery was inevitably precarious, an attempt to establish a family bond that the law refused to recognize. Enslaved spouses had no legal claim on one another or on their children. Jerry would not have been unusual in entering into partnerships that overlapped chronologically, especially if America lived at least part of the time in the next county.[6] Each woman testified later that she had been his sole wife and the mother of all his children, but they were speaking to government officials who couldn't be expected to understand the imperatives and traumas that had shaped their lives. So we don't know if the two women knew about each other. We don't know how either of them felt about Jerry or how he felt about them. We don't know if he was there when his children were born. We are not even sure exactly where America's son was born. She testified that he had been born on John Brown's farm in Bourbon County, and there was a Brown family living not far from the Skillmans and Tanners. We do know that an enslaved boy was born and recorded as David Tanner's property early in January 1861.[7]

Within weeks of the child's birth, most of the South would join South Carolina in seceding from the Union to form a new nation, founded, in the words of Confederate Vice President Alexander Stephens, "upon the great truth that the negro is not equal to the white man; that slavery subordination to the superior race is his natural and normal condition. This, our new government, is the first, in the history of the world, based upon this great physical, philosophical, and moral truth."[8]

In central Kentucky, not all slaveholders agreed with Stephens about the necessity for a new nation. They had depended on the United States to protect and promote the institution of slavery for generations, and they thought their best strategy was to continue to do so.[9] Kentucky remained in the Union. When the Emancipation Proclamation was issued in 1863, it freed only enslaved people in areas actively in rebellion, so its provisions did not apply in the Bluegrass. President Lincoln had moreover assured Kentucky slaveholders that, despite the proclamation's language, enslaved Kentuckians would not be enlisted in the nation's armed forces. But determined Black men streamed across the borders into Ohio and Tennessee, presenting themselves for service. By the spring of 1864, the Union began offering to compensate slaveholders for allowing enslaved men to enlist, and that June the government began an intense recruiting effort to get Black men into uniform. Any Black man, with or without the consent of his legal owner, would be accepted into service.[10]

On June 24, 1864, Jerry Burns and his friend Charles Skillman, who had been at his wedding to America, went to Lexington and enlisted in the Union Army. Burns was thirty years old, and the mustering agent described him as "copper" complexioned and about five foot seven. The army noted that the two men were technically C. C. Skillman's property and that he consented to their enlistment; he may have hoped that it would protect him and younger male family members from service.[11] Even if Skillman approved their departure, the journey would have been dangerous. Because Kentucky's slave codes, which legally constrained the behavior of men of color, were still in force, lawmen as well as vigilantes and Confederate sympathizers regularly arrested, assaulted, or murdered men on their way to enlist.[12] We don't know why Jerry Burns enlisted, but he must have been conscious of how many men like him were doing the same. More than half of Kentucky's enslaved men of military age joined the Union Army during the war, most of them that summer.[13] We don't know how he felt, but we have the words of some of the men around him. Elijah Marrs, who enlisted in Louisville two months after Burns, found his fear for his family almost too much to bear at his first daily muster. But when the sergeant called his name, he said, "I felt freedom in my bones, and when I saw the American eagle, with outspread wings, upon the American flag . . . the thought came to me, 'Give me liberty or give me death.' Then all fear banished."[14]

His friends said that Jerry Burns "never was sick or complaining but was always on duty and a good soldier and seemingly in the best of health," but almost immediately he came down with one of the infections and fevers common to Civil War camps. Admitted to the hospital at Camp Nelson, south of Lexington, he lingered for months. He died there in the fall of 1864. Later, no one in authority could even remember quite when his life had ended. He had been only one of so many dead.[15]

America was not with her husband when he died. She would later ask his friends to help her piece together his final weeks. But as the wife of an African American soldier, she was vulnerable to threats and attacks from Confederate sympathizers.[16] In the summer of 1865, Union General John M. Palmer announced that the military would issue passes to Black people that would allow unrestricted travel. It was freedom in its most basic form, and thousands of people took to the roads. They flooded into Lexington and the surrounding towns.[17] One of those people, in the turbulent wake of the war, was America Murphy Burns.

We do not know when she brought her son to Lexington, but we can make a good guess why she did. She probably hoped to join her siblings, who, like her, had been born there and remained close by. And Lexington might have seemed a more hopeful place than the surrounding areas. Between 1860 and 1870, the town's African American population more than doubled, until almost half of its residents were Black.[18] Because Kentucky had never seceded, it took the Thirteenth Amendment to free the enslaved people within its borders in the autumn of 1865, and the state was not bound by the terms of Reconstruction, which offered some forms of federal oversight and assistance to people struggling to leave bondage behind. Lexington was one of the epicenters of that struggle.

Black migrants to Lexington lived in cheap, previously undeveloped areas, many of them clustering on the eastern side of town, in enclaves owned by local white businessmen. Others squeezed into narrow lots fronting on side streets and alleys closer to downtown.[19] Within those cramped confines, America Murphy Burns would have hoped to secure the first prerequisite of a free life: physical safety for herself and her family. For central Kentucky freedpeople in the aftermath of the war, that was far from a certainty. The federal government had chartered the Freedmen's Bureau, a one-size-fits-all agency charged with maintaining order, rebuilding the economy, and protecting the civil rights of African Americans on the ground in the South. Bureau officials complained that they encountered more opposition in Kentucky than almost anywhere else.[20] The agents managed to document dozens of assaults, rapes, home invasions, and killings, but they couldn't stop them. General Stephen Burbridge complained in 1865 that "policemen and night watchmen who . . . are notorious woman whippers are permitted to go at large unmolested."[21] A third of the total lynchings recorded in Kentucky in the nineteenth century happened within a decade of the end of the Civil War.[22]

Like many other freedwomen in expanding Southern cities, America Murphy Burns did laundry to support her family. White middle-class women could afford to send out their laundry, and they were glad to do it. Laundering meant hauling gallons of water and mountains of soaked cotton and wool, scrubbing and boiling and agitating for hours, suffering burns and blisters from irons and lye. The work was desperately hard, but laundresses were independent contractors; America would have control of her own labor.[23] Easier access to her clients may have been one of the reasons that by the end of the 1860s, she was living on Upper Street, not far from the Fayette County Courthouse. That was where she lived in 1869 when she filed a claim on Jerry Burns's survivor's benefit. She explained some of her life to the army pension office in words that fit in the blanks on their forms. She told them about her marriage and her son. She failed to find the doctors who had treated her husband, but she got the testimony of Charles Skillman, who had enlisted with Jerry that day in 1864 and knew about his death, and her own sister Annie, who had been there when the baby was born. She presented herself to the government as a soldier's widow and a good mother. The nation would acknowledge her as an individual who was, in the formulaic words of the depositions, "reputable and entitled to credit."[24]

The daily work to build a free life, penny by penny, until dignity was an affordable luxury, was constant, but America kept doing it. The pension money—eight dollars for her and an additional two for the support of her son—added to her earnings and helped secure the deed to a narrow lot and house on Pine Street in downtown Lexington.[25] She, her son, and her younger siblings—

Annie, a few years her junior, and James, still in his teens—lived there together.[26] She was savvy and determined to take advantage of the new institutions of freedom. Only a month after it opened, she established an account in the Lexington branch of the Freedman's Bank, a new national institution designed to provide formerly enslaved people a place to secure their money.[27] When James was sixteen, he opened an account for himself, banking his earnings from his job as a carriage driver.[28] The two sisters continued to do domestic work. America's son, meanwhile, went to school.[29] He joined hundreds of African American students in Lexington, filing into classrooms their parents staunchly supported in the face of white opposition.[30]

When the Fourteenth Amendment was ratified in 1868, it offered a new vision of citizenship, rooted in due process and equal protection of the law. It was intended to be a negation of centuries of code and custom that had devastated families like America's. The abstractions of the amendment were inspiring, but in the house on Pine Street, she and her siblings and her son were making a life that grounded those gauzy aspirations in reality. A home, a family, a bank account, an education, a future. And because they did the work of making those ideas of citizenship real every day, the Murphys and their neighbors knew when those abstractions still fell short in practice. African Americans in Lexington held community meetings to call for change, to itemize the places where the legacies of slavery still survived in the crevices of the law in Kentucky.[31] Civil rights activists agreed that the best way to combat those legacies was to gain the right to testify in court against white people and the right to vote.[32]

Kentucky held firm against African American suffrage until the Fifteenth Amendment was ratified in 1870. The right to vote ostensibly meant equality in the political process for men, and voting could, at least in areas with larger and more politically active

Black populations, expand economic opportunity for formerly enslaved people and crack the legal codes that sought to entrench racial subordination. Both white and Black Kentuckians were well aware of the implications of Black suffrage. As the *Kentucky Gazette* assured its readers, it "would be a calamity justifying almost any measure to protect society from it."[33] Local vigilante and paramilitary groups terrorized potential Black voters and their families all over the Bluegrass. Black citizens begged Congress to take action. "We ... have been law-abiding citizens, pay our taxes, and in many parts of the State our people have been ... refused the right to vote; many have been slaughtered while attempting to vote. ... We appeal to you ... to enact some laws that will protect us, and that will enable us to exercise the rights of citizens."[34]

The memorialists sent their pleas to Congress because the Kentucky state government shrugged them off. There was no organized white supremacist violence in the state, the legislature insisted, and thus no need to act against it.[35] State courts would not accept Black testimony against white defendants, so the only place African Americans could hope for justice was in federal courts, which were empowered to take cases related to Black citizens' rights but were often inaccessible to Black plaintiffs because of distance or bureaucracy.[36] In 1871, when election officials announced that gubernatorial candidate John Marshall Harlan had won Franklin County by eight votes, shooting broke out in Frankfort. City police arrested a Black Republican activist named Henry Washington for the murder of two white men, and a white mob dragged Washington out of jail and hanged him and another African American prisoner. No one would admit to knowing anything about the perpetrators. But federal courts brought indictments against three prominent citizens.[37] The legislature quickly rewrote the law to allow for Black testimony in state courts, so friendly local juries could hear the case.[38]

In April 1872, the Supreme Court made sure that federal courts would no longer be a refuge for Black citizens. Four years earlier, two white men named John Blyew and George Kennard had been indicted in federal court in Kentucky for hacking the Foster family to death. Teenage Richard Foster had survived his injuries long enough to identify the murderers. The state of Kentucky challenged the convictions, and the Supreme Court ruled that, though the Civil Rights Act of 1866 gave federal courts jurisdiction in cases involving people denied their rights in state courts, that protection did not extend to witnesses. The Black victims were dead and beyond help, and the federal courts were not obliged to ensure that Black witnesses could testify about the crime. The case was sent back to the state courts, to be tried under Kentucky's new law allowing Black testimony, as was the case of the Frankfort lynchers, who were quickly acquitted. The federal judiciary had made clear that it would define the rights of citizenship for Black people as narrowly as possible, and the state government had learned that its best route to negate Black citizenship was through legal formalities.[39] It was a lesson they applied very effectively in restricting African American access to the ballot.

More than 750 new Republican voters added themselves to the Lexington rolls after the ratification of the Fifteenth Amendment, enough to have an impact in local elections.[40] In response, the city imposed longer residency requirements for voting, as well as a poll tax of $1.50. Those stipulations would disenfranchise about two-thirds of prospective new voters.[41] Men able to pay the new tax still faced the Citizens' Guards, a group of prominent white men who patrolled the town during elections.[42]

A Black bricklayer named William Garner, who lived in Lexington's third ward on the east side of the city, tried to pay his poll tax, but the tax collector, one of the leaders of the Citizens' Guards, refused his money. When he went to vote, Garner presented an affidavit that explained the situation to the officials at his polling place, in accordance with the provisions of the Enforcement Act of 1870, a federal statute intended to compel compliance with the Fifteenth Amendment. Two out of the three election judges present refused to allow him to cast a ballot and were charged with violating the law.[43] When the case came before the Supreme Court as *U.S. v. Reese*, attorney Benjamin Buckner, the founding commander of the Citizens' Guards, argued that rejecting Garner's ballot was constitutional, since his race was not the official reason for the denial. And the court's majority agreed: the Fifteenth Amendment provided no affirmative right to vote, merely the assurance that the right would not be denied explicitly on the basis of race.[44] *Reese* would be a permission slip to Southern cities and states to disenfranchise Black voters and Lexington a model for how to do it.[45]

Speaking at the dedication of a statue of Stonewall Jackson a few months after the decision, the Lost Cause apologist Moses Drury Hoge adamantly rejected the changes wrought by emancipation and Reconstruction. "If it be objected that we have already entered upon one of those political revolutions that never go backward, then I ask, who gave to anyone the authority to say so?"[46] Facing relentless attempts to reverse the progress of freedom and equality, Black people knew how precarious their gains could be. America Murphy Burns learned that lesson close to home. On Pine Street, the family's neighbors were Harrison and Matilda Williams; Harrison was a laborer, and Matilda took in boarders. Simon Williams, who may have been a relative of theirs, in turn lived with the Murphy sisters. In 1870, the census taker identified America as his wife.[47] Legal marriage would have meant losing the vital assistance of Jerry Burns's military pension, so, like many other couples of the time, the two may have made an informal arrangement, in which Williams was both partner and boarder.[48] But America found the lines defining her labor blurred. What work did she do for pay as a landlady, and what work should she perform for free out of dutiful affection? What was a loan, and what was a loving offer to help support the family?

Those arguments came to Fayette County Court when Simon Williams sued America Murphy Burns for nonpayment of a debt of $150. She countered that she had provided domestic services during the three years he boarded with her that were worth $200, and he hadn't paid her for them. Instead, they had lived as spouses, and he had promised to marry her, so she would be a wife in law as well as labor. Whether or not the two would actually have married and sacrificed the pension money, the promise might have felt like an important guarantee of commitment. Or maybe he had never made that exact promise, but America chose a way that the court would understand to express her feeling of betrayal. She, a woman who was careful with her money and her future, had cared for him without counting the cost, only to find that he had been keeping an account. Williams denied that he had ever said anything about marriage, though he acknowledged that at some earlier time *she* might have loaned *him* money. The case dragged on for years. In December 1873, America had to ask for a delay, because she was about to have a baby. It may have been Simon Williams's child, though that seems unlikely. He had left the Murphys' house in the summer of 1872; as her court filing put it, he had "deserted and abandoned her."[49] The baby was never mentioned again. In the spring of 1875, the court decided in Williams's favor and put the hard-won house on Pine Street up for sale to settle the debt.[50] America Murphy Burns left Lexington for Cincinnati, joining her sister Annie, who had moved a few years earlier; she would try to make freedom again in another place.[51]

———

But what was to be done about her son? When she had identified him to the pension authorities, he was an eight-year-old named after his father, Jerry. When he was ten, she called him Jerry again on her bank account application, then had the clerk cross that out and write in Isaac, the name he would go by for the rest of his life. He would later say he had been named for an uncle he had never met, perhaps a Murphy brother dead or sold away. We don't know when exactly his name changed or who chose his new one or why. It wasn't just his first name that was in flux. The pension office had recorded him as a Burns, but, when Simon Williams lived with the family, the census called him Isaac Williams, and that may have been the name his schoolmates knew him by.[52] A few years after that, he was old enough to go to work, as his uncle James had done. Where could his mother place him that would give him the security and hope she had worked so hard for?

She found the answer in her friends and neighbors. Eli Jordan was married to an old friend of hers, and she stayed with the Jordans, maybe when she first got to Lexington and maybe after she lost her home. Jordan had been training Thoroughbreds since before emancipation, and in the mid-1870s he worked for two men who stabled horses at the Lexington track, J. T. Williams and Richard Owings. It may have been through the Jordans that America got a job doing laundry for Owings. Williams and Owings also took her son on as a stableboy, beginning his education in the myriad demanding tasks of caring for a racehorse.[53] At some point, either J. T. Williams or Eli Jordan decided to try the boy in the saddle. As a twelve-year-old, he had his first ride on a yearling, who promptly threw him. The terrified child said he didn't want to get back on, but he finally did. Maybe he had already figured out that there was only one way to succeed at the work he had ended up in—pretending he wasn't afraid until he forgot to fear. He would hone his craft exercising the Williams and Owings horses in the morning, as well as continuing to imbibe generations of knowledge about how to maintain a Thoroughbred in top condition. When he turned fourteen, his mother let him travel to the races under Jordan's supervision, and his professional career really began.[54] He would remain not just a rider but a horseman for the rest of his life.[55]

The story of Isaac's first ride would later be treated as funny or sentimental, but it must have been terrifying in the moment. In 1878, a horse at H. P. McGrath's farm in Lexington suddenly bit his young groom's forefinger and lifted him off the ground, until the boy's weight ripped the end of the finger off.[56] That incident was recorded only because it was unusually grisly. Even the most mundane of tasks in a racing stable could end with maiming, and it took years to acquire the habits of calm and constant attention, quick and precise action, that marked a competent professional. Jockeying posed its own set of risks. When Isaac was starting out, a young rider named Frank Smith was unseated at the beginning of a race. His boot stuck in his stirrup, and he was dragged behind the horse and died of a fractured skull in minutes. His brother, also a jockey, had been killed in a race a year earlier.[57] "If there is any fear in a boy's composition," the racing commentator John H. Davis asserted breezily, "he has no business on a horse."[58] Instead of succumbing to fear, a jockey had to plan ahead to limit his risk and keep his horse balanced and under control, moving with the animal as they surged forward together. The job demanded tremendous core and upper-body strength and the ability to make decisions and act on them instantaneously. The best riders could also transpose a mental stopwatch on the landscape rushing by.[59] Boys like Isaac left their families to learn those skills; their companions were horses and horsemen, their lives constantly moving from track to track.[60]

America Murphy Burns would not have known all the pressures that would shape her son's life. But she must have had a more general set of concerns. Women like her had struggled since emancipation to protect their children from exploitative apprenticeships. She sent Isaac to work for Williams and Owings knowing that boys like him were vulnerable. She would have calculated the risk based on her own experiences with Owings and what she heard from the Jordans.[61] She would have weighed the presence of Eli Jordan, an older man, himself a father, who could care for her son and teach him skills that would give him a professional future. Isaac may not have remembered his father at all, and we do not know what he thought of Simon Williams. We do know that for the rest of his life he would call Jordan "the old man."[62]

Eli Jordan was obviously proud of him. "Isaac was always in his place and I could put my hand on him any time day or night. He was always one of the first up in the morning, ready to do anything he was told to do or to help others. He was ever in a good humor and liked to play, but he never neglected his work. . . . *He never got the big head.*"[63] Jordan introduced him to a trade that had a long history; Black men had been working Thoroughbreds in Lexington since before the first recorded race meet there in 1827.[64] We don't know what he taught Isaac—or if there was anything left to teach him—about the dangers of navigating debates over freedom and equality. We don't know if he spoke about what it had been like to be enslaved and what the boy heard about those years from his family. But we know Jordan gave him the gift he could, the gift of an occupation that generations of men like him had followed. He seems to have hoped it would be the basis of the conservative respectability that he wanted for Isaac—the boy who was always where he should be. In racetrack barns all over the South, the boy would be surrounded by skilled Black men. On the foundation of those centuries of expertise and the hopes of his mother and those like her, he would make his future, in a sport that was in the midst of a national revival.

In the decades before the Civil War, Thoroughbreds had been the treasured possessions of Southern plantation owners, who used the profits of cotton, sugar, and enslaved people to build the biggest tracks and offer the richest prizes. After the Civil War, the sport's epicenters of power migrated north, in part because, at a time when the war had helped to jumpstart new fortunes, racing retained its power as a marker of elite prestige. "Racing is the most expensive amusement in the world," mused a magazine correspondent in 1870. "It is a royal sport, beyond the reach of modest incomes; and . . . racing is adopted as a pastime by those who have riches and leisure, and who aspire to lead where the vulgar crowd cannot follow."[65] Plantation owners had seen in Thoroughbred racing a symbolic justification of their right to rule, and industrialists and financiers now used it for the same purpose.[66]

Saratoga had opened the doors of its track in 1863, building on its antebellum reputation as a vacation idyll. Soon high-class racing would come to New York City itself, courtesy of Leonard Jerome, whose daughter Jennie later married Lord Randolph Churchill and became the mother of the future Prime Minister. In 1865, Jerome, who had made his money in railroads and newspapers, bought 230 acres in what is now the Bronx and laid out a racetrack. When Jerome Park opened in 1866, members enjoyed a clubhouse that resembled a luxury hotel. But while Jerome happily sank thousands of dollars into this new project, he was also thinking bigger. In the winter of 1866, in his office on Exchange Place, he hosted the first meeting of the American Jockey Club, a new governing body that would not only rule Jerome Park but exert influence throughout American racing. The club, its power concentrated in the hands of fifty life members, included men from all over the nation, including former plantation owners, businessmen, and press kingpins. For president, Jerome tapped August Belmont, in deference to his prominence as a banker and Democratic Party power broker. Belmont, who had never owned a racehorse, promptly went shopping.[67] It was boldly envisioned, indeed. As the racing writer Joe Palmer observed decades later of Jerome's audacity, "No wonder Churchill would take a chance."[68]

It worked. General Ulysses S. Grant attended the inaugural meeting of Jerome Park in 1866, and the new track was on its way.[69] Racing might be run by aristocrats, but theoretically anyone could run a good horse, and race crowds were huge and came from all walks of life.[70] So the races, their supporters and supervisors insisted, were actually a great carnival put on by the wealthy out of benevolence and sportsmanship. If their horses happened to win most of the time, it just proved that their owners were men of discernment. The American Jockey Club was not merely a haunt for wealthy hobbyists. It was an occasion for the men of a new national upper class to prove that they had the resources and savvy to triumph against all comers, that they deserved the power they wielded.

Leonard Jerome had been a co-owner of the stalwartly Republican *New York Times*. August Belmont remained one of the most powerful Democrats in America. But that disparate past only underlined present unity. And that unity came from a mutual sense that if the world was changing, it must change properly. In the wake of the war, there was money to be made in railroads, in mining, in manipulating the stocks and shares of burgeoning industries. Whether or not the men in the American Jockey Club had agreed about slavery before the war, they were united in believing that this new economy had to be managed by and for those like them. As labor gained power in the 1870s, they increasingly feared and vilified labor organizers and strikers. To organize was down-right "wicked," probably the fault of "uneducated foreigners."[71] Northern businessmen and financiers speaking in those terms would have heard similar sentiments from Southerners insisting that Black men were congenitally lazy and Black women worked only as prostitutes.[72] The war had opened up new questions about what freedom meant, about what role working-class people and people of color had in the nation and in the marketplace, but a determined group at the top found that set of new questions so alarming that they had to be answered immediately and deci-sively. And in their club and at the track they could watch their preferred answers acted out, as their champions triumphed and reaffirmed their grip on power, before adoring multitudes.

By the 1870s, the wealthy of all regions could gather at Jerome Park, Saratoga, and Monmouth Park near the summer resorts of the New Jersey coast.[73] Meanwhile, Southern racing rebuilt. In 1875, Louisville unveiled its new track, Churchill Downs, and its new signature stakes race, the Kentucky Derby.[74] It was fitting that Louisville should have such a track, wrote the magazine *Turf, Field and Farm*, "as the metropolis of a great breeding state."[75] Churchill Downs, in other words, would be the display window for the work of Bluegrass Thoroughbred farms and their specialists. In racing's new landscape, the South, particularly Kentucky, would produce high-class horses, which would compete at regional tracks in Lexington, Louisville, Nashville, and St. Louis. The best of those would be cherry-picked for competition in the East.

The dazzling duels on the opulent new tracks might seem to prove wealthy men's right to rule, but the horses, just like the ones that had demonstrated the power of antebellum plantation owners, were the product of Black men's skilled labor. In the barns on the backside, a boy like Isaac worked in a community of Black mentors and friends. But part of his job would have been learning to navigate the frontside, the public areas of the track where spectators mingled. The track was, for months at a time, both his home and his workplace, and mastering the varying racial codes that governed different spaces within it must have been an anxious process. The more the boy learned of his trade, the more time he would spend on the frontside, where jockeys were expected to interact with colleagues, owners, fans, and reporters.

Isaac and jockey William Walker, only a year his elder, would be lifelong friends, and Walker must have provided much-needed advice not only about race riding but about the unspoken rules and perils of their profession. Walker had ridden at Jerome Park at the age of eleven and would vie for top Eastern prize money throughout the 1870s.[76] He rode the great Ten Broeck to victory in a famous match race in Louisville against the California star Mollie McCarthy, a contest mired in rumors of potential cheating. Right before the start, Churchill Downs founder Meriwether Lewis Clark, Jr., had shown Walker a tree and said, "if you do not ride to win, a rope will be put about your neck and you will be hung to that tree yonder . . . *and I will help to do it.*" Terrified, Walker, who thought his horse might not be healthy, tried to back out, but Clark refused even to let him speak.[77] In the photograph we have of him as a child, Walker crosses the competent hands that guided his winners and stares out with what looks like exhaustion in his eyes—already tired of calculating so many risks so young.

In 1877, Walker would ride Kentucky Derby winner Baden Baden, trained by another Black horseman, Edward Brown, about ten years Isaac's elder. Brown had won the Belmont Stakes, along with other prestigious prizes, as a jockey and had lived only a few blocks from the house Isaac grew up in. Closer to the Lexington track, near Eli Jordan's home, lived Ansel Williamson and Oliver Lewis, who trained and rode Aristides to win the first Kentucky

William Walker at about the age of ten. His jockey's cap signals that he was already a professional horseman. Kentucky Historical Society, SC 1246.

Derby in 1875. Along with Brown at the Lexington track were other young Black trainers, like Isaac's dear friend John T. Clay. Clay had started out as a jockey, but after an accident he left the saddle and instead became a successful trainer.[78] Abe Perry, about the same age, was already launched on a training career that would take him to the Derby winner's circle with Joe Cotton.[79] Dudley Allen, who had joined the 5th U.S. Colored Cavalry only a month after Jerry Burns enlisted, mustered out of his war service as a sergeant in 1866; by 1875, he was an established trainer, on his way to working two Kentucky Derby winners.[80] This was the community in which Isaac grew to manhood.

Isaac was fourteen in May 1875 when he saw Volcano, the horse that had thrown him as a yearling, finish second to Aristides in the first Kentucky Derby. But his only mount of the meeting finished out of the money.[81] Finally, in September 1876, at his home track in Lexington, he chalked up a winner, piloting a two-year-old filly named Glentina to outlast a big field of talented horses, including Baden Baden, who would go on to win the Kentucky Derby the next year. In the results, his name was listed as Isaac Burns and his weight at about ninety pounds.[82] Only a few days later, he would win at Louisville, this time with the two-year-old filly Spring-branch, owned by Williams and Owings. This time, he carried the name he would have for the rest of his public life: Isaac Murphy.[83]

Murphy spent 1877 and 1878 paying his dues, and, when he got the breakout chance that jockeys dream about, the chance to ride a good horse, he took advantage of it. The big bay colt Vera Cruz, the star three-year-old of the Williams and Owings string, was Murphy's first Kentucky Derby mount and his first ticket away from the local and regional races in Kentucky and Tennessee and to the glamour of Saratoga and Jerome Park.[84] Williams and Owings dissolved their partnership in 1877, and Eli Jordan changed jobs and brought Murphy with him. Their new employer was J. W. Hunt Reynolds of Fleetwood Farm in Frankfort, Kentucky, thirty miles from Lexington.[85] It was with Fleetwood horses that Murphy would ascend to the dizzying heights of national celebrity.

In the fall of 1878, Murphy was second in the Colt and Filly Stakes for two-year-olds at Lexington, so he got a good look at the back end of the winner. That was Spendthrift, a light chestnut with a big white star, compact and well-muscled. Edward Brown was working the colt for Daniel Swigert and had shaped him into a talent that impressed the railbirds.[86] The horse drew national attention, particularly from Eastern owners who had a job in mind for him. Pierre and George Lorillard, scions of the tobacco dynasty, shot, yachted, and dined with famous skill and passion, and they had turned their attention to horse racing with equal assiduity. They seemed so impossibly overstocked with the best horses that, in the words of an immemorial track complaint, the parity of racing itself was in danger.[87] In January 1879, Swigert sold his star for the hefty sum of fifteen thousand dollars plus a cut of future earnings to an agent for "some person or persons of New York City who are forming a new racing stable."[88]

The temporarily anonymous buyer was James R. Keene, who would go on to be one of the most significant figures in the history of the turf. Keene was emphatically a man of the new economy. Coming from England with his parents as a child, he grew up in California and worked odd jobs until, in the 1870s, he provided horses and mules to the Bonanza Mine. He took his profit to San Francisco, where he found his true calling on the stock exchange. Before the Civil War, corporations were by convention assumed to be chartered for specific purposes that fulfilled a public need. After the war, they were public in the sense that they could sell stock on the open market. The business of buying and selling that paper, of making it multiply and transforming it into money—that was a line of work that brought in billions to Wall Street. And when he moved to New York, Keene was recognized as a virtuoso at it. He served as a consultant to tycoons like J. P. Morgan and John D. Rockefeller in handling the fluctuations of their companies' stocks.[89] A reporter described his "characteristic attitude . . . standing by the ticker . . . his eyes fastened on the narrow paper ribbon . . . his heart-beats attuned to the clicks." This was a new kind of rich man, the writer mused. "He will leave many millions to his family, but not his name to a railway system. And because he . . . helped to make the richest and most 'practical' nation in the world go stock-mad . . . he must remain one of the conspicuous figures of that momentous period of our financial history."[90]

Keene's purchase paid off. Spendthrift won both the Belmont Stakes and the Jersey Derby in 1879, and he stormed into Saratoga that July as the favorite in the Travers, the great summer stakes race for three-year-olds. But Kentucky visitors seemed eager to side with J. W. Hunt Reynolds's Falsetto. The colt hadn't run at two, but when Eli Jordan started working him, he "knew he had a race horse."[91] Isaac Murphy rode him to a battling second in the Kentucky Derby, and they went on to take the Clark, still one of Churchill Downs's great stakes, with ease. The big dark brown colt was clearly first-class, and his rider kept firing in winners that spring, until the papers proclaimed him the best jockey in the West.[92] Then the stable shipped to Saratoga to meet the best horses and jockeys of the East.[93]

Handicapper and turf historian Walter Vosburgh later described watching Falsetto move over the track. His stride was "as regular as the piston-rod of an engine and as resistless as fate. The halo of victory seemed to shine about him as he galloped low-headed and with frictionless bounds that marked him among" hundreds of horses.[94] When Travers Day arrived, hundreds of people flooded in to see him and Spendthrift. Both had only been defeated once, but Spendthrift had beaten Lord Murphy, who had beaten Falsetto in the Kentucky Derby. What racing people call a formline thus seemed to favor Keene's colt, but paddock bettors, the people who stake their money based on an animal's physical appearance, looked at Falsetto and thought they had never seen "a more perfectly ordered horse." At the start, all five competitors "shot like flying rockets at midnight." Spendthrift's stablemate Dan Sparling took the lead, letting Edward Feakes on Spendthrift settle in second. The pacemaker rattled off fast fractions to try to run the competition off their feet over the mile and three quarters. But Murphy was too canny for that and settled Falsetto into a comfortable rhythm, dropping him out the back of the field and waiting for Spendthrift. When Feakes made his move and took the lead, Murphy moved with him, coming level with the rest of the horses. He bided his time for a furlong and then shook Falsetto up and sent him for home. As he shot past the field and took aim on the leader, "the whole grand stand absolutely groaned with excitement." Feakes went to his whip, but it was too late. Murphy won by almost three lengths, riding with hands and heels. "I cannot describe the scene which followed," admitted one reporter, as the crowd exploded. The eighteen-year-old jockey hadn't been given any instructions. He had decided to keep his horse in striking distance, lull Feakes into a false sense of security, and then use the power he had kept in reserve to sweep to victory. Everything had been planned and executed meticulously. "Murphy," summed up the reporter, "is one of the best jockeys in America. He is very observant . . . quick to perceive the weak points of an adversary, and prompt to take advantage of them. He has a steady hand, a quick eye, a cool head, and a bold heart."[95]

Two weeks later, the two horses faced each other again in the Kenner Stakes. This time, Murphy followed Spendthrift when he took the lead and stayed close, the two horses "moving like two steam engines." Then Murphy went to work, and Falsetto won by four lengths. One Kentucky spectator laughed, "We bet these people blind to-day."[96] The results were in, the press concluded. Falsetto would reign as "'King of the Turf.' Let him wear the diadem in peace."[97] Pierre Lorillard seized the opportunity to reassert his dominance and bought Falsetto for eighteen thousand dollars, more than had ever been paid for a three-year-old colt in America.[98] At home in Frankfort, they claimed that the corn on Fleetwood Farm came out that year in red and white kernels, to match the stable's colors in jubilation.[99]

That August, Isaac Murphy was nationally famous and at the height of his profession. In Lexington that same month, his mother, not yet forty, died of rectal cancer.[100] Years later Murphy would tell a version of his life story to a reporter in St. Louis. The printed interview never mentioned his mother. It said his father's name had been Jeremiah Burns Murphy.[101] Maybe the reporter reflexively thought in terms of fathers' legacies to sons or took down the story wrong. Nineteenth-century newspapers were not scrupulous about fact-checking. The attorney L. P. Tarlton, who had known the jockey for years, got the names right when he wrote Murphy's obituary. He explained that the boy had started riding under the name Burns and switched almost immediately to honor his grandfather, Green Murphy, who had been proud of his career as a jockey.[102] But Green Murphy was dead by the time Isaac started riding.[103] It's certainly possible that they discussed his potential future, but we don't know that they ever did. The result of these stories is the same in the end. They erase America Murphy Burns or relegate her to the background in the new world her son lived in professionally, a world in which mentors, friends, employers, and colleagues were all men. Her story didn't fit there.

Maybe Isaac Murphy didn't like or didn't know how to talk about her and her name, the name that he took permanently at the age of fifteen and made internationally famous. Better to leave his feelings about his mother to silence. But even silent, she had made sure he was recorded in the end.

CHAPTER 2

———

"He Had Famous Flyers to Ride Then"

IT ONLY TAKES one good horse, horsemen like to say. But that's to get to the top; to stay there takes more than one and a grim determination to succeed. Murphy had the determination. In 1880, a year after his triumph with Falsetto, he was living on or adjacent to Fleetwood Farm, a nearly seven-hundred-acre estate two miles outside Frankfort. He lived next door to Eli Jordan and his second wife Belle and his grown daughters Lizzie, Tillie, and Ella. In the winter, Murphy would have worked preparing the young horses for competition and sale, pitching in to help with mares and foals. The women in Eli Jordan's household may have fed him. They would have been used to having teenage jockeys and grooms underfoot.[1] When the thaw came, the men and boys would start exercising the racehorses to get them fit.[2] In late April, the racing circuit heated up, and the stable usually shipped first to Nashville; then back to Lexington; then to Louisville; to Latonia, near Cincinnati; and to St. Louis. In July, they continued west to Chicago and from there back east to the late summer heat at Saratoga. In August and September, the New Jersey and New York tracks traded racing dates, and an enterprising jockey was expected to hop from one to another. As autumn came in, it was back to Latonia and other meetings closer to home. Essentially, Murphy and his colleagues lived out of suitcases and on trains from April to November. In later years, he could take the train in the evening from Lexington and arrive in New York the next night, a foretaste of today's jockeys' travels by helicopter and transcontinental airplane.[3]

A horseman worked in many of the biggest cities of nineteenth-century America, but he usually didn't see much of them. Andrew Jackson, who came from Kentucky as a jockey, remembered spending months at Jerome Park but seeing New York only twice: once when he went into town to buy a suit and once to eat in a restaurant on Fourth Avenue.[4] Stable staff slept in dormitories, and big stables traveled with their own cooks. Prominent Black horsemen did sometimes stay in large hotels or boardinghouses; at least in some cities, their celebrity allowed them to contravene local practices about segregated accommodations. But they often took advantage of the services of families who rented space to other African American travelers.[5] Murphy boarded in Saratoga with a Black woman named Maria Dangerfield.[6] At Derby time in 1886, Murphy and his friend, the trainer Abe Perry, stayed in Louisville with Sarah Wrightson, who worked as a laundress.[7] In some cities, such arrangements may have been his only option; in others, he may simply have preferred not to be alone among white hotel guests when he could stay with friends or with women who might remind him of his mother. But even in places that felt like home, he was always on the road.

He was always tired, but, like most successful jockeys, he was not afraid, because he couldn't afford to be. Everyone got hurt. It was only a question of when and how badly. And he was extraordinarily lucky. He always remembered what he called his worst accident, the day at St. Louis when the horse in front of him fell and brought Murphy's mount down with him. One of the horses in the pack struck him as it was going by—an inch to the side and he would have gotten a hoof directly to the head—but he managed to drag the other jockey, who was badly injured, away from danger. He rode the next race. In interviews, he never even mentioned the time his stirrup leather broke on the way to the post. His horse threw him, and he fell on his head. He remounted and rode the race, finishing second, before he had to be helped off the course.[8]

The real battle, the one he had to think about constantly, was with his own body. When he first started riding, he weighed about seventy pounds, which was ten pounds lighter than a two-year-old would be asked to carry in spring.[9] The weights horses carried in races varied according to their age and the distance run. And the weight a horse carried had to include not only the rider but his saddle and bridle. The weights were a constant source of debate throughout Murphy's career, with Western and Southern tracks typically mandating slightly lower imposts. New York turf authorities pressed to bring three-year-old weights up to 115 pounds throughout the nation, and Lexington, Murphy's home track, adopted approximately that rule in 1881, while Louisville stuck to 110 pounds for three-year-olds and 105 pounds for two-year-olds. When younger horses ran against older, they still received massive weight allowances, with two-year-olds carrying between eighty and eighty-five pounds and three-year-olds between 102 and 107.[10] The punishingly low weights meant that many jockeys were children and teenagers, and advocates for higher weights argued that their inexperience was more likely to lead to accidents or breakdowns than a few extra pounds on a horse's back. Besides, experience produced slyer riders, master tacticians;

keeping them out of the saddle was a loss for the sport.[11] In the end, those voices would win out. Today's top U.S. jockeys usually weigh around 110 pounds, with top Europeans a few pounds heavier. Their struggles are still agonizing. The immortal Lester Piggott famously summed up, "I have lived on black coffee and cigar smoke all my adult life."[12]

Murphy's battles with his weight started almost immediately. The spring before he rode Falsetto, who carried 118 pounds in his races at Saratoga, Murphy weighed in at 130. To ride all the horses Fleetwood wanted him to mount, he'd have to lose about twenty-five pounds, and he would still have to leave some of the younger horses to his lighter colleagues; he was a bulky elder statesman at eighteen.[13] As his metabolism slowed, he would pack on more weight each winter, and every spring brought a harder struggle to lose it, followed by months of desperate work to keep it off or to lose more for a particular race. Some of those bouts made national news, like when he went from 124 pounds to 111 in thirty-six hours.[14] He doggedly insisted that, if necessary, he could ride at 105, though he would usually aim for 110.[15]

Murphy acknowledged that his regular diet for half the year was mostly fruit, with occasional tiny portions of meat. A small piece of dry toast was a treat. On race day, to sweat off excess pounds, he walked and ran for miles wearing heavy sweaters. Afterward, he would sometimes beg for water as he collapsed. But once all that liquid had poured out, it couldn't be replaced, or the weight would return. Primitive saunas and homemade laxatives could take off a few extra pounds quickly in an emergency. The only time he didn't feel sick was when he slept, so he often went to bed before it was dark. And in that condition, he pointed out, "you get on the back of a big, active thoroughbred racehorse that is full of life and ambition, and sometimes is vicious besides, and you are expected to control him and ride him in such a manner that his best speed will be obtained for a long distance." No wonder that at the end of a race he shook.[16]

He could only do it because he was strong. He had the steely core that is a jockey's most essential asset, the muscles that keep the rider balanced and steady even as the horse gallops under him. He rode in a world in which whips and spurs were much more common and carelessly used than they are now, but by the lights of that world he was a delicate and coaxing rider. He was "a great conservator of a horse's powers."[17] That meant that much of what he did was done with small cues, a muscle and bone conversation with his mount. These are the subtleties that make a great jockey. Charlie Elliott, who rode twenty-nine Epsom Derbies and won three, mused, "You can talk about strength and balance and having good hands and a good seat . . . but at the end of the day there's a bit of a mystery. There's something strange and marvelous happens between the horse and certain men who get on his back and you can't explain it. You can only demonstrate it."[18] Murphy demonstrated it.

Not everyone appreciated it. Throughout his career, he was one of the jockeys—with a peer in every generation—that people grumbled waited too late. Jimmy McLaughlin, Murphy's closest rival, usually liked to be toward the front and had a noted talent for "hustling" a horse, while Murphy usually preferred to sit quietly. He was one of the only "really artistic" jockeys in America, judged some reporters.[19] His horses were there at the finish, but they usually didn't make the pace, and they didn't sail away from the pack. Many of their finishes were squeakers. One oft-circulated tale insisted that owner E. J. Baldwin, watching Murphy ride one of his horses, had chewed tobacco feverishly during the race, as the horse galloped well in the rear. When Murphy got his mount into the lead at the finish, Baldwin had to hand his tickets to a friend to cash so he could go home. He'd swallowed his plug of tobacco.[20] (Murphy later confirmed the story "with modifications.")[21] Even if many owners might have found his technique nerve-wracking, others would have commended it. Then and now, the connections of a handicap runner find that a decisive victory just means more weight to carry next time. Bettors liked to complain that finishes like the ones Murphy rode could give a man a heart condition, but, after all, as his supporters pointed out, his instructions were to win, and he won.[22]

Falsetto had been Murphy's breakthrough mount, but he had been sold. As the lead jockey for Fleetwood, he had access to other good horses, but the situation abruptly turned precarious when J. W. Hunt Reynolds died suddenly in the fall of 1880.[23] His wife Meta immediately announced that she planned to continue breeding and racing.[24] But her husband's friends, while carefully sympathetic, recoiled at the thought of a woman officially running horses at their tracks. In 1881, the Fleetwood horses were listed with Eli Jordan as owner. Everyone would have known that was an administrative fiction, but it soothed the feelings of racing men reluctant to welcome a woman.[25] Murphy rode Fleetwood horses successfully on the usual circuit in the years between 1880 and 1883.[26] He had always been able to pick up rides in races where Fleetwood didn't have an entry, supplementing his income with the fees he negotiated on a case-by-case basis for those mounts. But now he found himself looking a little harder for rides, as Mrs. Reynolds shifted to focus more on breeding than racing. He rode some good horses for friends like Edward Brown and Dudley Allen, both already established young trainers.[27] But he also took the mounts he could get, and some were good—like Kentucky Derby winner Leonatus, with whom he sometimes partnered—and others mediocre.[28] In 1883, his winning percentage was about thirty-nine, which was superb, though not unmatched. The even more remarkable achievement was the 75 percent of the time in his career to that point that his mount was in the top three. Even if he couldn't get a horse up to win, he could pick up some purse money, suggesting that he was getting the best out of all his mounts, not just benefiting from the luck of riding good ones.[29] But in absolute numbers, he rode about half the horses McLaughlin and other top jockeys did. He was paying the cost of increasing weight and, more than that, of riding for a stable that was small and getting smaller.[30]

J. T. Williams often tried to secure the right to Murphy's services when Mrs. Reynolds didn't command them.[31] Abe Perry, a friend of Murphy's, was training for Williams, so it was once again the community of his childhood that supported the young jockey.[32] And in the Williams barn was one of the great and durable racehorses of the age. Checkmate was a big, brown gelding, tough-mouthed and tough-minded. In later years, when the horse was in trainer James Rowe's barn, bystanders used to worry he'd pull Jimmy McLaughlin over his head and kill him. ("Jimmy is a strong boy," Rowe shrugged.)[33] Murphy and Checkmate seemed unbeatable at any track and any weight. They won at Saratoga, at Long Branch, at Louisville; they won in stakes races and handicaps, with Checkmate sometimes carrying twenty-five pounds more than his closest competitors.[34] When they won the Dixiana Stakes at Louisville in 1882, defeating Kentucky Derby winner Hindoo, the newspapers said Murphy rode "with a confidence sublime in its grace. He felt his horse, and rested satisfied that . . . he was astride of the greatest of them all. . . . A rocket couldn't have mated him, and with the roar of 5,000 excited voices . . . he burst under the deciding wire, without whip or spur."[35] Falsetto might have been Murphy's breakout horse, but Checkmate was the horse who made his career.

In 1883, Mrs. Reynolds remarried to prominent attorney and

racing enthusiast L. P. Tarlton, who would run Fleetwood into the twentieth century.[36] But Murphy quietly announced in the *Kentucky Live Stock Record* early that year that he would be available to other owners to ride in stakes races.[37] It was a short entry in a long column of small print, but it held great significance. He was testing whether he could make a freelance career or negotiate a new deal with another employer. He was experimenting with the kind of free labor bargain his mother would have understood and appreciated—selling his skill in the open market.

Marriage may have affected his calculations. He and Lucy Carr got married in January 1883. Lucy and her mother Susan Osborn lived on Washington Street, one of the main thoroughfares running through downtown Frankfort. Lucy had been born when her mother was in her teens.[38] Her father, Adam Carr, was not with the family by 1870, when the census recorded Lucy living with her mother, another Black woman named Matilda Foster, and a houseful of other children. It's unclear if or how the people in the house were all related; what is clear is that Susan Osborn and Matilda Foster kept those children through their domestic work and probably some assistance from their neighbors, Granville Lewis and his wife Fanny. Lewis was a veteran who had a steady job as a laborer, and, by 1880, Susan and Lucy had moved in with the Lewises and were recorded as stepdaughters of the family, working as laundresses and house servants.[39] In the photograph we have of Lucy, she is almost ethereal, dressed in a lace-collared, puffed-sleeve blouse and gazing at the viewer with soulful eyes. At the wedding, held in her home, she wore satin and brocade. The groom's cake featured a candied figure of Murphy on Falsetto, and the guests included some of his track friends, including Edward Brown, William Walker, and other jockeys. Surely Eli Jordan was there as well.[40]

At their marriage, Isaac had just turned twenty-two, and Lucy

Lucy Carr Murphy. Kentucky Historical Society, MSS 167, Box 4, Folder 3.

may just have turned eighteen.[41] She was a teenager, and he was already nationally famous, but there were experiences that they shared. Murphy had lost his own mother, but he would live with his mother-in-law for the rest of his life—another woman probably born in slavery near Lexington who supported a family by doing domestic work, in a small enclave of other Black families. Her daughter had been raised to her trade, in the same way his mother might have raised him, had he been a girl. And Lucy had been reared to be respectable, in the same determined way America Murphy Burns had raised him. Among their friends and neighbors, they would have heard constant reminders that a wedding was a marker of commitment that separated Black people from the time of slavery, when neither of their mothers had been able to marry legally.[42] When Murphy traveled for work, his wife came with him, which seems to have been unusual and a potential measure of their devotion to each other and their marriage.[43]

The Murphys never had children, which, given the long periods of time they were together, may suggest difficulty conceiving. But they remained a closely knit family of adults. In the fall of 1883, they bought a house on Megowan Street in Lexington for five hundred dollars.[44] It was a milestone in the life of freedom Murphy's mother had set out to build for their family. He was a husband, a householder, and a respected man in his community. And he would now seek to cement his place in his profession, selling his highly prized skills in a national market.

When Murphy officially changed employers, the contract negotiations became public. For an African American retained rider on a Kentucky farm, such arrangements were cloaked in assumptions of mutual obligation and affection. Edward Corrigan was not a man who dealt in affection. The newspapers could not decide quite what Murphy's salary would be as Corrigan's top jockey, but they pegged it somewhere between two and five thousand dollars a year (equivalent to between half a million and a million and a half dollars today).[45] He could also make his own arrangements to take outside mounts in races where Corrigan didn't have a horse. The Turf Congress, which governed many Western tracks, firmed up custom into rule in 1883 and announced standard fees: a winning jockey had to be paid twenty-five dollars and a loser ten. When an owner grumbled to the press about having to pay a minimum fee, a jockey wrote to the *New York Sportsman* to suggest dryly, "Perhaps your correspondent has never ridden in a race. If he has not I should advise him to try it when there is a big field, and perhaps he will alter his opinion."[46] Most jockeys cobbled together a living from per-race fees and tried to maintain ongoing relationships with particular trainers and owners that could help those fees add up. The regularity and sheer size of Murphy's salary put him alongside a very few other men at the top of his profession.

Ed Corrigan had come up as a railroad laborer and then a contractor to railroads.[47] A formidable figure for decades, he swung his weighted cane at anyone who irritated him.[48] He broke the jaw of a reporter for the *Kansas City Times,* because he said the paper had insulted his integrity and his brother's personal appearance. Then he hunted down the editor, because, he said, the man had threatened him with a pistol. "Now, I don't like to have a fellow around looking for me with a gun, so I just knocked him down and took it away from him."[49] But Corrigan took his racing seriously. He hired top-notch professionals and invested in good horses and in the infrastructure of a first-class stable of the late nineteenth century, like his specially designed railroad car, sixty feet long, to carry his stock to the races.[50] Murphy had clearly chosen an employer eager to make his mark nationally. And in 1884, the jockey would establish himself long-term at the top level of his profession.

The Kentucky Derby, first run in 1875, had grown into a significant race, but the very insistence on its prominence suggested just how local it still was. "Every year the interest in the Kentucky Derby increases," the *Spirit of the Times* observed hopefully.[51] For the Derby of 1884, Murphy had the mount on Buchanan for William Cottrill of Mobile, who was one of the last remaining stalwarts of the antebellum Southern turf. Cottrill's trainer was the veteran Bill Bird, born of free African American parents in Nashville.[52] Murphy had ridden Buchanan to a stakes victory as a two-year-old, and Cottrill and Bird were eager to get him back aboard.[53] But in a prep race that spring at Nashville, the horse ran away with his rider, and Murphy announced he wouldn't take the mount in Louisville. Riding a potentially dangerous horse for a stable he wasn't connected to long-term was a professional risk he understandably didn't care to take. But Cottrill announced that he wouldn't release Murphy from their prior agreement, which meant that, even if he forced Cottrill to put up another jockey, Murphy still wouldn't be able to ride in the Derby, and it was a big enough race for him to grit his teeth and go through with it.[54] Buchanan was fitted with blinkers, and Bill Bird had him in perfect condition, "fit to run for a man's life, as they say," in front of the biggest crowd Churchill Downs had ever seen. Murphy held the horse steadily near the back of the pack. As the race progressed, he let Buchanan ease forward, picking off his rivals. Murphy didn't touch him with his whip as they sailed to victory. A few days later, they came back and won the Clark Stakes. Buchanan was clearly a good horse, though to prove he was a great one, he would have to tackle better competition, the racing writers said. And, pronounced the *Spirit of the Times*, that "contingency will hardly arise at Louisville."[55]

These days, when we mark the milestones of Murphy's career, that first Derby win is a big one. But the real star he rode that week in Louisville was in the Kentucky Oaks, the contest for three-year-old fillies, where Ed Corrigan's Modesty tore away from the field and powered home in front by six lengths. Murphy had sweated to ride her at 105 pounds, but it was worth it.[56] She was a granddaughter of Reel, one of the greatest race mares on the antebellum turf, and would be in her turn the great-grandmother of Regret, the first filly to win the Kentucky Derby. Like Regret, she was a big chestnut filly with a white blaze, and her bravery and toughness were easy to see. It was Modesty who would take Murphy to what his contemporaries regarded as a far more significant Derby victory than the one in Louisville.

That June, Washington Park, the opulent new track at Chicago, kicked off its inaugural meeting, as the Democratic National Convention met in town. With so many trains running to the city, the promoters boasted, they would have larger crowds than any in the history of American racing.[57] The members of the Washington Park Club, the leading citizens of the rising city, were said to be worth, all told, some three hundred million dollars.[58] The meeting's cards were full of big purses, including the boldly named American Derby. Most tracks had a Derby—Louisville, St. Louis, Latonia. But the American's name was commensurate with its ambition. In the late nineteenth century, it drew horses from all over the country and was "one of the grandest outdoor sights to be seen in America."[59]

In that first American Derby, Modesty took on the colts, carrying a seven-pound penalty as a stakes winner. Murphy kept her just behind the two leaders. When he saw a hole between them, Modesty quickened to get through it, but the gap was a tight one, and the filly ended up squeezed between her two rivals. Then, on her outside, a horse swerved sideways and bumped her. But she

American Derby Day at Washington Park, Chicago, 1893.
Murphy won the first three runnings of the event, which was called
"one of the grandest outdoor sights to be seen in America."
Keeneland Library Thoroughbred Times Collection.

stayed on her feet and regained her stride, sticking her neck out at the line to win by inches and earn national acclaim for herself and her jockey.[60]

In 1885 Murphy's fame would skyrocket to new heights. He finished the year with a 38 percent strike rate, placing him at the elite level of his profession, though he followed his established pattern of taking only about half the mounts of his closest rival for supremacy, Jimmy McLaughlin.[61] Murphy struggled to make weight, so he rode selectively. He could afford to wait for a stakes race and know he would have a mount that would be there at the finish. Ed Corrigan could usually supply those horses, and that spring and summer Murphy rode reliable stars like Modesty and Pearl Jennings. But sometimes his stable failed, as it did that summer, in the second American Derby. Corrigan's Irish Pat was his logical entry but didn't seem up to the competition, so Corrigan yielded to the request of E. J. "Lucky" Baldwin of California, who had shipped his Volante to Chicago and was hoping Murphy would ride him. Fifteen thousand people turned out on a muddy July day to see Murphy keep Volante to the back of the pack, looking well beaten as the leader stretched out by four lengths. But with half a mile to go, Murphy began picking them off, and suddenly the crowd realized just how much horse he had left under him. He ran down the leader and finished a length in front, in what the papers described as a dazzling display of jockeyship. Baldwin paid Corrigan fifteen hundred dollars for Murphy's services, and Murphy himself got an additional thousand.[62] Almost immediately, the press reported a rumor that Baldwin had signed Murphy as his lead jockey, paying him an annual salary of five thousand dollars, a thousand more than Corrigan (the equivalent today of adding a few hundred thousand dollars to a paycheck moving up toward two million). California would soon be a formidable rival to the East, as Western horsemen opened their checkbooks to secure the best trainers and jockeys. "It looks very much," judged the *Spirit of the Times,* "like the Californians want blood, and they will get it."[63]

Baldwin must have wanted it all the more at Saratoga that August, when Volante went up against Corrigan's Freeland in the Excelsior Stakes. This time Murphy was in the saddle for his employer, and Volante led all the way, until Freeland passed him and won easily, in a classic Murphy ride.[64] Freeland's mother, Belle Knight, had come from a community of Shakers in Ohio to be bred to the great stallion Longfellow at Frank Harper's Nantura Farm in Midway, Kentucky. When Harper presented his bill for board and care for the mare, which amounted to $150, her owners said they couldn't pay it, and he ended up instead offering them ten dollars and taking the mare in trade. She produced a series of high-class racehorses, but the best was the angular brown gelding with the white face.[65] Freeland was in the money in twenty-one stakes races in the course of his career, sometimes carrying dozens of pounds more than his rivals.[66] Those grueling years of campaigning told on his legs, until Corrigan's trainer J. W. Rogers monitored the horse's soundness "with a care only shown elsewhere by the young wife of a high-living Anglo-Indian general who has not arranged to leave a jointure to his widow."[67] Murphy reckoned that when the horse was race fit, "he was a tough customer. . . . Had he lived in another time he would have been a four miler."[68] The men who had taught Murphy his trade, men of Eli Jordan's generation, had come up on the racetrack at a time when to win at four miles was the benchmark of true greatness. To make the comparison was to judge Freeland a worthy successor to the stars of the past. He was "not beautiful," summed up the *New York Tribune*.[69] He was gawky and lanky, but he was brave and stubborn, and in full stride he moved with inexorable grace. And in a few short weeks in the late summer of 1885, he and Murphy rewrote turf history.

A great champion demands a great opponent, and Miss Woodford was that. Well into the 1950s, men who had seen them all said she was the greatest filly ever. Bred at Runnymede Farm near Lexington, she went east as the property of Mike and Phil Dwyer, who were spending their Brooklyn meatpacking fortune at the track. She would go on to win thirty-seven victories in forty-eight starts and become the first American Thoroughbred to earn over a hundred thousand dollars in purse money. She won at distances from a mile and an eighth to two and a half miles, an unheard-of display of versatility. When she retired, she was shipped to California for broodmare duty, but the train wasn't really necessary, turf writer Kent Hollingsworth would later muse. "She could have run from Saratoga to, over, and beyond the Rockies."[70]

On August 10, the two horses met in the Champion Stakes over a mile and a half at Monmouth Park in a clash of titans. Jimmy McLaughlin and Miss Woodford made the pace, with Freeland stalking. Murphy timed his move with icy precision, and right at the wire Freeland surged forward to win by a length. Eight days later, the Dwyers sent their mare into battle again in the Special Stakes, this time at a mile and a quarter, and the two horses ran together through the stretch, until Murphy shot Freeland through a gap on the inside and went under the wire first by a neck.[71] Immediately, Corrigan and the Dwyers agreed to a match race to be run forty-eight hours later, at the same distance.[72]

Murphy thought the race would come too soon, that his horse should have more time off.[73] He could have used some himself. In August, there were multiple tracks running in the New York area, and he had hopped a train Tuesday night to Saratoga, spent Wednesday there, and come back to New Jersey that night to ride the match race on Thursday. He had also had to lose five pounds vary rapidly to ride another race, and he made himself so sick he couldn't keep food down.[74] He stayed flat on his back until he had to mount Freeland. The race unfolded in what had become typical fashion, with McLaughlin and Miss Woodford in the lead, Murphy and Freeland gaining slowly through the stretch. The crowd groaned and roared; Corrigan froze; Pierre Lorillard leaped to his feet and craned his neck.[75] The two horses flashed under the wire together, and this time she had won. When Miss Woodford came off the track, "such an ovation it was as might have shamed the triumphal entry of a Roman general." The crowd cheered as if she were Henry V after Agincourt or Wellington after Waterloo, the reporters gushed.[76] Both the winner and her rival had made themselves immortal. "Their names will not be forgotten while the turf is kept up in America."[77]

Three weeks later, the Dwyers were ready to try again, to prove that their mare's victory had been no fluke. Her trainer, James Rowe, this time essentially said what Murphy had: she needed time off. The Dwyers held firm, and he quit.[78] When the arrangements were made, Corrigan immediately sent a telegram to Murphy in St. Louis, where he was riding, and told him to drop everything and get to Brighton Beach, where the race would be held.[79] People flooded in on "every mode of conveyance running" to see Murphy and Freeland come from behind once again and this time romp home four lengths in front of Miss Woodford.[80]

As autumn came, Murphy had reached a new pinnacle in his career. He had raised his strike rate to almost 39 percent, the best of any jockey that year by a considerable margin.[81] Racing periodicals and businesses featured endorsements from him and pullout posters like the ones sports magazines would continue to print for decades.[82] But he feared for his health if he continued to try to maintain a weight below 115 pounds. He suggested that he would begin riding independently, contracting for select rides on a case-by-case basis. But there was that contract he had supposedly signed with Baldwin. Shortly after Freeland's final victory over Miss Woodford, the two men announced that they had come to an agreement. Murphy would ride for the Californian for one year only, for six thousand dollars.[83] Surely he could push his body for one more year, especially to earn the equivalent of about two million dollars today.

Early in 1886 Isaac and Lucy Murphy set off across the Rockies. They rode the train to San Francisco and stayed at the Baldwin Hotel, a jewel of E. J. Baldwin's real estate empire, as Isaac worked horses at the Baldwin farm and rode races at the Pacific Blood Horse Association meeting.[84] The California crowds shouted their approval at seeing the celebrity on the track.[85] California by the 1880s had a whole colony of Thoroughbred breeders and owners. Only a few years earlier, Eadweard Muybridge had photographed railroad baron Leland Stanford's horses, pioneering technology that would help to lay the groundwork for California's signature industry, the movies. Baldwin, Stanford, financier James Ben Ali Haggin, and George Hearst (father of William Randolph Hearst) lavished money on their stables, their barns adorned with silver and crystal.[86] Black men from the South, including the virtuoso blacksmith John Isaac Wesley Fisher, who had been eight at the time of emancipation, staffed Baldwin's Santa Anita, 54,000 acres tucked at the base of the San Gabriel mountains. Fisher always remembered when Murphy came to California and offered pointers to the younger men about riding.[87] One of them was Fisher's son Julian, who hoped to become "the next Isaac Murphy."[88]

Thousands of miles from home, Murphy would have found the people and the routines of the barn familiar. He was probably more comfortable with them than with Baldwin and the patrons of the Baldwin Hotel, where he and Lucy were very likely the only African American guests. Instantly recognizable in his big black hat and long black coat, Baldwin was "a kind of small, solemn-faced, stingy-looking version of Mark Twain."[89] He was, judged one contemporary, "a good hater."[90] A serial husband, he was the subject of gossip in the nineteenth century; in the twenty-first, he would be the object of investigations. His second cousin, Verona Baldwin, later testified that he regularly told young women he could help them financially, then blackmailed them into sex. He had, she asserted in the language of the day, "used [her] criminally against [her] wishes." She would have left him alone if he had left her alone, she said, but he hadn't. So she ambushed him in the Baldwin Hotel and shot him.[91] Baldwin continued his behavior, answering a fan letter that a little girl named Lillian Ashley wrote to one of his racehorses. He continued writing to her until she was almost twenty, when she visited him in California. When she arrived, he offered to adopt her and then to marry her (though he was already married). When Ashley had Baldwin's baby, he denied that the child was his, and Lillian's sister Emma shot him. "I thought it was my Christian duty to kill him," she told a court during her trial for attempted murder.[92]

Murphy and Baldwin had nothing apparent in common. But as a professional, Murphy got from Baldwin exactly what he wanted. Looking back on that period in his career, one reporter reflected, "he had famous flyers to ride then."[93] The first of those was his old friend Volante. Murphy won with him at San Francisco during his trip to California.[94] Over the next few years, they would win at Louisville, Kansas City, Washington, D.C., and Saratoga.[95] In New Jersey in August 1886, the pair beat the Kentucky Derby winner, Ben Ali, at the Derby distance (in those days a mile and a half), giving the younger horse fifteen pounds.[96] When Volante won the Columbia Stakes in Chicago, the local newspapers judged him "now the sensational animal of the West."[97] In 1886, Murphy would ride Baldwin's Silver Cloud to his third consecutive American Derby; he was still the only rider ever to have won the race.[98] A few days later, Baldwin offered Murphy a new contract for the following year, paying him ten thousand dollars for his services as stable jockey. With the addition of whatever rides Murphy picked up in races where Baldwin didn't have an entry, the reporters figured his income would total about fifteen thousand dollars, which would run to about four and a half million today.[99] In 1887, stable and jockey continued from strength to strength, though Murphy missed out on his fourth consecutive American Derby riding Goliah, who didn't quite stay the distance.[100] The real star of 1887 in the Baldwin stable was in the two-year-old crop. His name was Emperor of Norfolk.

When the Emperor came into the paddock, with Murphy aboard, "everyone fell in love with him." At two, the bright bay looked older, a throwback to the rugged four milers of the past.[101] The horse campaigned relentlessly. He won three consecutive races in Chicago, then reeled off victories at Saratoga, Jerome Park, Brooklyn, Coney Island, and Kansas City.[102] Murphy sacrificed his body to ride the lighter weights that summer two-year-old races demanded, so he could partner the young champion.[103] The following year, the Emperor started as a winner and kept winning, first at Nashville, then at Brooklyn, Jerome Park, and Coney Island.[104] But his greatest achievements were at Chicago that June.

The Emperor went off as the favorite in the 1888 American Derby.[105] Murphy, as usual, kept his horse to the rear. As the leaders tired each other out, Murphy finally let his mount ease forward, and "the gallant colt shot past" them and won stylishly.[106] During the Chicago meeting, he would win two more stakes, the Drexel and the Sheridan, in effortless fashion, before he was retired.[107] In 1889, Murphy called him "the best I ever saw, and I hardly believe it possible to breed a better one." The Emperor wasn't just fast; he could lead or come from behind, and he never stopped trying. "I have faith that I will live to ride some of his colts to victory, as I believe he will prove as successful in the stud as he was on the turf."[108]

The Emperor died in 1907. In his final hours, horsemen gathered to mourn, until he seemed like "a dying monarch surrounded by his court."[109] Almost a hundred and fifty years after his American Derby win, his line lives on through his great-great-granddaughter Mumtaz Mahal, herself a Royal Ascot champion, who produced a slew of influential progeny. Through her, Emperor of Norfolk is in the pedigrees of two of the greatest sires in the history of the Thoroughbred, Bold Ruler and Northern Dancer.[110] Murphy didn't ride the Emperor's colts. But he was right about what his descendants would accomplish.

By the time he rode the Emperor, Murphy had ascended to not just national but international fame. The press most often compared him to Jimmy McLaughlin in professional status, but in style he was usually paired with Fred Archer, one of the greatest jockeys in the history of British racing. Often, he got shorthanded as "the colored Archer" or "the black Archer." In 1887, the *Chicago Tribune* acknowledged the validity of the comparison: both men liked to ride a waiting race and often won in a close finish. But Murphy rode a more diverse book of mounts to a similar level of success, which argued sharper skill. Why not call Archer "the white Murphy"? Murphy was not Archer's imitator, but his American equivalent; had not Pierre Lorillard himself supposedly offered him a hefty salary once?[111]

Lorillard was the arbiter of the comparison because he was Archer's most famous American employer. In 1881, the tobacco scion had fulfilled the dream of generations of American racing men when he sent his colt Iroquois to England to train for the Epsom Derby, first run in 1780, the model and namesake of every Derby in the world. Archer had already won the Derby twice, and, with him in the saddle, the American upstart went off second-favorite at 11–2. Epsom, which first held races in the seventeenth century, is a U-shaped turf course rather than an American-style dirt oval, and the Derby begins with an uphill run, followed by a left-handed bend going back down toward the final half mile. That bend sharpens into the famous Tattenham Corner, an acute downhill turn that requires a beautifully balanced athlete, a horse that can corner on a slope with the precision and power of a sports car. Archer kept Iroquois tight to the rail around it, and the horse showed his class as he stormed down the hill, cruising past the leader to win by a neck.[112]

The news got to New York around eleven in the morning. At Jerome Park, where it was a race day, it was shouted through the barns. On Wall Street, the Stock Exchange closed. Reporters mobbed Pierre Lorillard's house.[113] He wasn't at home; he was at the Union Club with friends, celebrating the wedding of Leonard Jerome's daughter Clara the next day. When the ticker at the club announced the result, the groom scolded Lorillard: why on earth wasn't he at Epsom?[114]

Archer's fame had transcended the racetrack in England. "Archer's up," said Londoners, when they meant that they could take care of something easily.[115] But fans on both sides of the Atlantic knew that ease came at a price. Both Archer and Murphy were meant to weigh almost 150 pounds and had to weigh under 120 to do their jobs.[116] Archer, like Murphy, usually sweat off twenty-five or thirty pounds that he put on in the off-season, and he regularly drank a purgative mixture concocted especially for him. A friend once swallowed a tablespoon of it and ended up in bed. Archer gulped it down by the glass. Sometimes the very sight of food so nauseated him that he literally ran from it.[117] In 1884, his wife suddenly went into convulsions after delivering their second child and died. Archer stopped sleeping or leaving his house. He started talking about suicide.[118]

When Archer recovered, he seemed to do so with a vengeance. In 1886, he won the English Triple Crown aboard Ormonde, a son of Bend Or, on whom he had also won the Derby. Perhaps it was the very sweetness of the achievement that made it so painful, the racing writer Christopher McGrath speculates. He might have hoped a horse like Ormonde could save him from his depression and found, ultimately, that no horse could.[119] He agreed to ride in the Cambridgeshire Handicap that autumn and managed to get down to 119 pounds for the occasion, but the effort weakened him, and he contracted typhoid. His sister, who was taking care of him, was looking out his bedroom window when she heard a noise. Turning, she saw him holding a pistol she had no idea was in the house. She screamed and struggled with him, but he silently looped his arm around her neck, put the gun in his mouth, and pulled the trigger.[120]

The papers immediately rushed out editions with the news, and London busses stopped to let passengers read the headlines.[121] At his funeral, on a gray November day, the shops closed in Newmarket, Suffolk, where Archer, like generations of British racing men, had lived. The town turned out to watch the coffin pass. The grandees of the English turf had sent flowers, as had Pierre Lorillard, whose arrangement included two small American flags and the inscription, "in memory of achievements in which America has shared."[122] At the end of 1886, when the figures were totaled up, Archer had, for the thirteenth consecutive year, the highest winning percentage of any jockey in England.[123] In life and even more in death, Archer exemplified the allure and the danger of being a jockey, the reverence it inspired and the horrors it could drag into a man's life. He reminded racing fans that their heroes were mortal, that they struggled under pressures that could be crushing. Isaac Murphy already knew that.

CHAPTER 3

———

"I Ride to Win"

THE DAY MURPHY AND Emperor of Norfolk won the American Derby, Frederick Douglass was also in Chicago, attending the Republican National Convention. That afternoon, he became the first Black person to receive a vote for the presidential nomination of a major party. Addressing the convention to chants of "Douglass, Douglass, Douglass," he argued that Black men like Jerry Burns had proven their allegiance to the nation. That allegiance must be repaid with a guarantee of the rights of citizenship.[1] But with guarantees in short supply, Black people found themselves constantly called upon to prove that they deserved the rights extended on paper in the Constitution. Murphy lived daily with that imperative.

In the spring of 1889, he told a reporter that he made as much from outside mounts as he did in salary (bringing his earnings up to twenty thousand dollars annually or the equivalent of between five and six million dollars today). "I am as proud of my calling as I am of my record," he asserted, "and I believe my life will be recorded a success, though the reputation I enjoy was earned in the stable and in the saddle."[2] He made his living by physical labor in a sport that moralizers deplored, but that labor demanded tremendous technical skill and physical sacrifice, and he resolutely insisted that both his work and his character were irreproachably respectable. Where he came from, both the work and the insistence would have been well understood.

As an adult, Murphy lived in a community that jealously guarded its respectability and its children's prospects.[3] His colleagues and his neighbors were often the same people. In Lexington, almost half of the horse trainers in the city were Black, and so were more than half the jockeys. They clustered near the track, sometimes in the African American neighborhoods that had sprung up since the Civil War.[4] They proudly saw themselves as hard-working, deserving professionals. They were the ones who would make the new future America Murphy Burns had not lived to see.[5] Her son took the next step toward her dreams when he and Lucy Murphy purchased property on East Third Street, adjacent to the Lexington track, for ten thousand dollars.[6] They would live there, in a "handsome and commodious red brick" house, for the rest of Murphy's life.[7] A few years later, they bought a lot near Gratz Park, one of the oldest neighborhoods in downtown Lexington, as an investment.[8] In 1890, Murphy joined the Lincoln Lodge of Masons.[9] Black Masons announced themselves in their communities as men of substance, men of whom their friends and families could be proud.[10]

But striving to prove oneself worthy of respect, even if it fostered personal and community pride, was no guarantee of safety. In the 1880s, Murphy would have seen that in the case of John Bush, a Black man from Lexington. Isaac Van Meter, Bush's employer, shot his own teenage daughter, then told police that Bush had killed the girl because she had broken off an affair with him. Bush was tried and convicted for her murder by an all-white jury but successfully appealed his case to the Supreme Court, which ruled that racial discrimination in jury selection was unconstitutional. Bush's attorney before the Court in Washington was L. P. Tarlton, Meta Reynolds's new husband. In 1884, Bush was retried, this time without explicit racial restrictions on jury selection. He again faced an all-white jury, which again convicted him and sentenced him to death. This time, there was no successful appeal. The Bush case thus threw into sharp relief one of the most pressing questions of the period for Black citizens: whether de facto forms of oppression would slot in seamlessly to replace de jure ones.[11]

In 1883, the Supreme Court heard a cluster of cases challenging racial discrimination in public accommodations. It ruled that the government had no authority to police such discrimination by private citizens. The Court drew a distinction that it argued was validated by long tradition: Black people had attained freedom, but that did not entail the right to equality in their daily lives. In any case, white citizens did not seem to require protection against discrimination, and the Black man was not entitled "to be the special favorite of the laws."[12] The court thus voided the Civil Rights Act of 1875, the most direct precursor to the 1964 law, a crown jewel of the modern civil rights movement. John Marshall Harlan was the sole dissenter. Frederick Douglass mourned the law's death. "It told the American people that they were all equal before the law; that they belonged to a common country and were equal citizens. The Supreme Court hauled down this flag of liberty in open day, and before all the people, and has thereby given joy to the heart of every man in the land who wishes to deny to others what he claims for himself."[13]

Shortly before the 1883 decision, Douglass spoke at a convention of thousands of Black men in Louisville, gathered to discuss what the future might hold.[14]

Thus in all the relations of life and death, we are met by the color line.
... It hunts us at midnight; it denies us accommodation in hotels and
justice in the courts; excludes our children from schools, refuses our
sons the chance to learn trades. . . . While we recognize the color line
as a hurtful force, a mountain barrier to our progress . . . we do not
despair. . . . When we consider how deep-seated this feeling against us
is; the long centuries it has been forming; the forces of avarice, which
have been marshaled to sustain it; how the language and literature of
the country have been pervaded with it; how the church, the press, the
play-house, and other influences of the country have been arrayed in
its support, the progress toward its extinction must be considered
vast and wonderful.[15]

Douglass acknowledged how high racism loomed in all aspects
of American culture and suggested just how creative and resilient
Black people would have to be to move that mountain. But he
believed they could do it, in part because they had already accom-
plished so much. He pointed to what he called "self-made men,"
his iteration of an old American archetype that he saw in formerly
enslaved people and their children. They had to "acquire their
education . . . amidst unfavorable conditions, to hew out for themselves a way to success, and thus to become the architect of their
own good fortune."[16] He was talking about people like Isaac Murphy and his neighbors. They were Douglass's proof of concept. At
scale, repeated throughout the nation, their work could establish
that equality was not only just but attainable and beneficial for a
whole society. That meant that men like Isaac Murphy were not
just significant in their own communities but as symbols, characters in stories of achievement.

Douglass had watched his son Charles play third base for the
Washington, D.C. Alerts in the years after the Civil War.[17] In his

study, he hung a picture of the Black boxer Peter Jackson and explained his logic to surprised visitors: "Peter is doing a great deal with his fists to solve the Negro question."[18] Jackson came to the United States from Australia in 1888 in search of a heavyweight title fight. He never got a chance—John L. Sullivan refused to fight a Black man, and Jim Corbett did the same, once Jackson fought him to a sixty-one-round draw. So Jackson demonstrated his steely determination and slippery prowess on heavyweights who did get in the ring with him, like Pacific Coast fighter Joe McAuliffe.[19] Jackson convinced even reluctant editors and community leaders who had previously seen boxing as degrading that the ring could be a theater for Black advancement.[20] The greater the prestige of Black athletes, argued the *Cleveland Gazette,* "the quicker our importance as a race grows with all classes of people in this great and peculiar country."[21]

Athletic competition seemed to offer a potential resolution to problems implicit in the argument that respectability would command white people's admiration and their consent to full Black freedom and equality. In a world without the Civil Rights Act of 1875, appealing to the nation's sense of fairness seemed to many Black people a futile endeavor. Moreover, framing the issue that way meant giving legitimacy to assumptions of Black inferiority, implying that citizenship was a privilege many Black people might not deserve and not a right they were all entitled to. That argument could divide African American communities along lines of class and occupation.[22] While men like Murphy and Peter Jackson might be mindful in their own lives of the demands of respectability, their exploits appealed to Black bettors in bars as much as they did to Black commentators in parlors. And when they went to work, they did not convince white people they deserved to win. They won.

Jackson, who said that he had enjoyed visiting with Murphy

at the track in Chicago, commended him as one of the "most distinguished men" of his acquaintance.[23] And he noted that Murphy's occupation allowed more scope for achievement than his own. Sullivan could refuse to meet Jackson and thus stymie his quest for a title, but, Jackson asked, "Why don't McLaughlin or [Snapper] Garrison refuse to ride in a race because Isaac Murphy has a mount in it?"[24] Jackson's point was that such a refusal was unthinkable. Murphy rode against them all, and he beat them all.

In Chicago, prominent members of the Black community organized a party for Murphy in 1886. "To say that Mr. Murphy is a lion does not half express it," the papers reported. The party, to be held at the grand Sherman House Hotel, would feature a ball and a performance of *Richard III* by a company under the direction of the African American actor Charles Winter Wood. "Mr. Wood is now studying to put a new shading to the lines: 'A horse! A horse! My kingdom for a horse!' which he intends to render as a delicate and special compliment to the guest of the evening."[25] Murphy represented all the artistry and accomplishment of Black people, presented in high style, a style that could help sustain people as they scaled the mountain of the color line.

Black fans certainly believed that Murphy offered an example, in his own quiet way, of a formidable cool. In the days when Murphy was riding Freeland, he ran into a young white man, who asked how good the horse was. Murphy, who didn't like giving specific information about his horse's condition to individual bettors, especially in public, gave him a polite non-answer. The boy followed him and kept pressing him, this time in an insulting way. Murphy "looked him full in the eye for a moment, and then turned calmly away from him, at the same time bisecting with a blow of his whip a fly that was crawling over his boot." He couldn't act out his anger at having some arrogant brat treat him like the help. But he made it clear that he was a professional who didn't have to put up with it, either. That icy control, that exquisitely calibrated swipe of the whip, said that, and the Black grooms in the paddock knew exactly what they were looking at and laughed with glee. As one chortled, "Isaac opened the blade to cut him dat time."[26] That casual rendering of dialect made the story into minstrel-adjacent humor for white readers. But we can still see the pride Black on-lookers and fans could take in a man who was as constrained as they were but who could silently look a white man in the face and say, without a word, that he demanded respect.

But, inspiring as it could be, Murphy's position could also be precarious and painful. He had lived part of his adult life in African American–dominated spaces, where Black friendship and Black expertise were the rule, but he also knew what it was like to be the only Black man someplace, to be treated with careful joviality or careless ridicule. As far as we know, he and Lucy stayed at the Baldwin Hotel without any difficulties, but a few years after their stay, the manager admitted that the hotel's unwritten policy was not to accommodate Black guests. He explained, "the line is drawn in a delicate way, so as not to give offense or to render the manager liable to the law."[27] In a segregated world, Murphy could some-times be the exception to the rule, and being an exception must have been exhausting. When Peter Jackson stayed at the Baldwin, he was forced to take a room in a rear annex, which enraged San Francisco's Black citizens. "Didn't he shake the hand of the Prince of Wales?" demanded one man indignantly. "Ain't he the best fighter in the world?"[28] Even as Murphy's own life meant con-stantly calculating where he was, how he looked, and what people thought of him, his very success and his presence, like Jackson's, raised a central question about the nation. How could a society hold these men up with gushing adulation on one hand and deny their right to citizenship in the most basic sense—their ability to

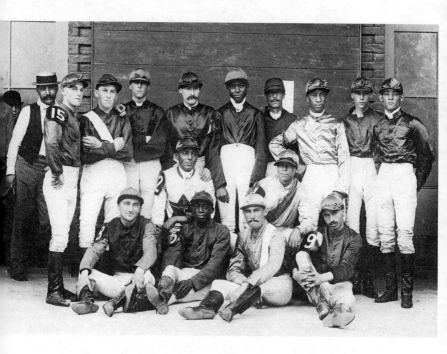

Jockeys at Sheepshead Bay, 1891. Murphy is in the second row on the left.
Keeneland Library Hemment Collection.

travel unimpeded and on equal terms with others—on the other?
Surely that fundamental contradiction must be resolved.

In New York, Murphy and his colleagues sat for a typical jockeys' room portrait. Black and white men crowded together casually. George Taylor rested a hand on Murphy's shoulder, while Murphy propped a forearm behind Tony Hamilton's head, and Fred Taral, next to Hamilton, smiled boyishly. These were the kinds of pictures Frederick Douglass hoped to see, pictures of a nation that could be dreamed into being, that could be shown and then made real.[29] Murphy's gaze angled away from the camera, seeming to see that new world.

———

But, like his stay at the Baldwin Hotel, much of Murphy's ability to demonstrate his skill and to inspire the hopes of Black Americans depended on his access to good horses and to the good graces of the men who owned them. And that meant dependence on wealth that dwarfed his own. Like a modern professional athlete, his power always existed in proximity to greater power. What kind of new world did the men who employed Isaac Murphy dream of?

Murphy had been feted in Chicago, the site of some of his greatest triumphs, a city that boasted that its hinterland was everything west of the Alleghanies and south of the Mason Dixon line.[30] "As in London we find men whose business field is the world, so in Chicago we find the business men talking not of one section or of Europe, as is largely the case in New York, but discussing the affairs of the entire country."[31] Visible first as a dark cloud that railroad passengers could see on the horizon, Chicago was a place where the realities of America's new economy were being lived and debated and bled over.[32]

The horses Murphy rode to victory in Chicago were the prizes of a new kind of Western wealthy men, manipulators of the new economy. E. J. Baldwin had always had an eye for the possibilities of new transportation and infrastructure technologies. Born in Ohio and raised in the Midwest, he went into the grocery and hotel business, then shipped grain by canal to St. Louis and Chicago. In the 1850s, he went west, figuring to provide domestic goods to California towns and mining colonies. When he arrived in San Francisco, he got a brickyard contract with the government for military buildings on Alcatraz Island and put his profits first into real estate and then into mining, where he cashed in on some of the richest strikes of the day, including the enormous Comstock silver lode. That money bought Santa Anita, an agricultural paradise, where, he said, "from hill to hill, and as far as the eye can reach is mine, and on that ground we raise everything but mortgages."[33] He could see a future of Western agribusiness, powered by oil, electricity, and vast irrigation projects.[34] In the census, he described himself for decades as a "capitalist."[35] In addition to Southern Black workers, Baldwin staffed his agricultural empire with Latino immigrants, who were paid intermittently in goods and grudging infusions of cash. Chinese immigrants also worked on the ranch in substantial numbers, because, Baldwin proclaimed, white laborers wouldn't "go to work . . . for a dollar or a dollar and a half a day."[36]

Baldwin's turf rival, Kentucky-born James Ben Ali Haggin, came to California from New Orleans in the 1850s to practice law. But Haggin quickly figured out that the most reliably lucrative place to be was behind the ledger that recorded the loans that funded the mighty extractive enterprises of the West.[37] He learned early that "technical mastery in an unmitigated mess of courts and debt could build a machine for churning wealth."[38] The most famous of Haggin's investments stemmed from his relationship with Irish immigrant Marcus Daly, who started as a miner and ended up a mine owner. Daly decided that a seemingly played-out silver mine in Butte, Montana, could yield a rich vein of copper and convinced Haggin and his associate George Hearst to invest in the mine once he had purchased it. The men already owned more than 150 mines all over the Americas, raking in millions in profits from all kinds of ore, as the spider-webbing of railroads through the West in the 1880s meant that the metals could be shipped in bulk for processing.[39] But Daly's find, the Anaconda mine, would be the richest of their investments, ultimately accounting for 20 percent of world copper production. Copper was the metal of the future, the material for telegraph, telephone, tram, and electric wire.[40] The partners would, by the 1890s, own not only the mine but the ore processing facilities, the lumber reserves, the water resources, the real estate, and the transportation networks that undergirded the success of the Anaconda. The local and state governments, over which the Anaconda "loomed . . . like a monstrous leviathan," often seemed to be subsidiaries of the company.[41]

Haggin would ultimately turn his industrial logic—economies of scale, control of every aspect of the production line—to his Thoroughbred farms, first at Rancho Del Paso in California and then at Elmendorf Farm outside Lexington, where he helped to invent the sprawling nurseries of today's Bluegrass.[42] Baldwin, Daly, Haggin, and James R. Keene practiced a new set of customs for wealthy men in America; they made their money in Western industries but often invested it in the East. They joined Fifth Avenue clubs, summered at Newport, worked on Wall Street, shopped at Tiffany's, and ate at Delmonico's. They were part of a flourishing postwar American upper class, enmeshed in mutual interests and understandings.[43]

The annual membership booklets of the American Jockey Club in the 1880s included many of them. August Belmont remained president, with Leonard Jerome and William R. Travers, another denizen of Wall Street and the namesake of the Travers Stakes, as vice presidents. Other members might as well have been listed alongside the industries with which they were synonymous: Andrew Carnegie (steel), A. J. Cassatt and E. H. Harriman (railroads), Pierre Lorillard, Jr. (tobacco), H. O. Havemeyer (sugar). Then there were the Roosevelts and the Van Burens, the scions of New York politics and society, and Ward McAllister, its social arbiter.[44] Havemeyer would later testify before the New York legislature that, even though the American Sugar Refining Company essentially controlled the price and supply of all refined sugar in the United States, the company didn't *mean* to do it. In 1895, the Supreme Court would rule that the Sherman Act, the U.S. government's initial attempt to control the bottomless appetite of conglomerates like American Sugar, could not regulate manufacturing since that only occurred in one place at a time. State governments would bear sole responsibility for regulating massive businesses, with supply, transportation, and ancillary interests all over the nation, which practically meant they would be unregulated. John Marshall Harlan, the sole dissenter, wrote to a friend, "The greatest injury to the integrity of our social organization comes from the enormous power of corporations."[45]

Harlan had plenty of evidence of the dangers of unlimited wealth and its concomitant, unlimited poverty. In 1882, when Isaac Murphy first began to write his name in the smoke of Chicago, more than half of all the children born there would die before they were five.[46] American miners, whose work enriched men like E. J. Baldwin and J. B. Haggin, died twice as often as those in Germany and the United Kingdom, and they died not just in accidents but of chronic, job-related illnesses.[47] American workers organized—or tried to. In 1886, a campaign for an eight-hour workday in Chicago factories ended in an explosion in Haymarket Square that killed at least eleven people. Labor organizers who had held the rally at Haymarket were sentenced to death. Who would benefit from someone's labor? What did it mean to be equal before the law? What freedoms did the United States guarantee? These were new iterations of questions that would have been familiar in the house on Pine Street where Isaac Murphy grew up; they were the questions that Americans fought over with desperate directness for his whole life.

The sporting press was full of think pieces that reflected the anxieties of the age and anecdotes that revealed how racing fans responded to them. The *Kentucky Live Stock Record* in the early 1880s insisted repeatedly "that we should like to see the day when there is not a colored individual in the borders of Kentucky."[48] The very presence of Black people was toxic to economic growth and public safety, because "with few exceptions, they are ignorant, indolent, dull, improvident, and any thing but enterprising citizens."[49] They were biologically unfit for citizenship. And so, rather than guaranteeing their rights as citizens, the state should instead use its power to keep them away from white people.[50] These sentiments were published in journals that explicitly denied a political stance; they were supposedly only articulating the needs and best interests of farmers and stockmen, men who for generations had depended on skilled African American labor. In 1883, *Turf, Field and Farm*, geared to the same audience, posed itself as explaining a well-known truth to outsiders. "In every ex-slave-holding State, negroes . . . are found who enjoy a higher reputation for veracity and other virtues than some officious meddlesome fellows whose skins are white. . . . It is the character of the individual, not his color, which gives weight among the neighbors to his statement."[51] So how to reconcile that worthiness of respect with sweeping generalizations about erasing whole communities? The trick was to understand, to believe implicitly, that every Black man worthy of such respect was an exception and constantly on probation. And Isaac Murphy played a starring role in stories that fostered this cognitive dissonance.

In the summer of 1880, J. W. Hunt Reynolds gave Eli Jordan a gold pin, inscribed with his name. Below it was engraved, "for faithful service."[52] As long as white owners and fans could see in African American horsemen, even the famous ones, the virtues they associated with fidelity and subordination, they were willing to extend them professional autonomy and even acclaim. Meta Reynolds told the papers, "Of course I tell you of Isaac's honest and trustworthy nature, for the whole of the American turf must be cognizant of that fact; but no one knows it better than I do."[53] That simple statement could bloom into a whole field of subtexts. The newspapers insisted that he loved Mrs. Reynolds because she had taught him his letters and his manners.[54] A few shifts in emphasis, a few careful word choices, a few half-truths or lies, and a young man raised and educated with the fruits of his mother's labor in the heart of a Black community became the petted protégé of a white patron. The *Spirit of the Times* cited a Kentucky trainer to drive home the point; he always used Black stable help, he explained, because, "When a nigger's bad, he'd d—d bad; no doubt about it. But sir, when a nigger is attached to you and yours, all the money in New York couldn't make him sell you out."[55] Murphy could function as a latter-day version of a faithful slave and soothe the sensibilities of white fans.

And if those reassurances failed, newspaper readers could always turn to the words of Jack Chinn, who raised and raced horses in Lexington and knew Murphy well. Murphy rode some great finishes for him, including on his Kentucky Derby winner Leonatus and the stakes winner Ban Fox. The pair took the Horse Traders' Stakes at St. Louis in 1885, a victory Chinn must have particularly savored, because he was one of the great horse traders in Kentucky history.[56] Chinn was famous both for his knife (which he stuck into a bookmaker at Latonia in 1888) and his sharp eye for a man ready to buy.[57] There ought to be a monument to Jack and his son Phil, one horseman reflected, for, between them, they created a market for Thoroughbred yearlings that "took more tobacco farmers from behind the plow than the International tractor."[58] Chinn's stock in trade was his status as the ultimate insider, the man who knew the codes and could translate them. And he had a store of Isaac Murphy stories. "You know how Isaac talks," he'd start, before reeling off some phrases in dialect.[59] People who had only read about Murphy or only seen him ride—the vast majority of Americans—didn't know, especially because most reporters recorded him in the monosyllables of a craftsman interrupted at work or rendered his speech in polished, careful periods. But now they could believe they knew that he talked like something out of a minstrel show. So they could choose. He was either special but subordinate, or he was safely inferior. They could paint all the blackface they wanted on to him and not worry about what rooting for him meant about whether Black men were worthy of respect and of citizenship.

Those worries might have felt particularly urgent because of what Murphy represented. When the handicapper and turf writer Walter Vosburgh praised him as "graceful as an Apollo," a genteel and irreproachable professional, he literally embodied a possible future, a possible present, where Black men could be the epitome of grace and style, worthy of admiration and emulation.[60] Murphy was accruing the proper trappings of middle-class life, according to the press. Lucy Murphy herself was often depicted as one of those accoutrements. When reporters described her, she appeared as part of the backdrop, quiet beside her husband. Her silence was a measure of her propriety for the press's audience. Even more important than her silence was her face. Sometimes she was described as "quadroon," other times as "a beautiful octoroon."[61] She was "a woman of evident education and a great deal of refinement, being as easy in her manner as any lady."[62] Lucy Murphy was a beautiful, very light-skinned woman, but portrayals of her were about connotation as much as depiction. Decades of popular culture had acclimated nineteenth-century white Americans to the idea that mixed race women could be accepted as beautiful and refined. Lucy had "scarcely a taint in her blood," a British newspaper reported, saying more directly what American newspapers usually implied: her appearance and behavior *almost* entitled her to be treated with the respect due a white woman, because she was "almost white."[63] Murphy himself they described as "bright copper."[64] The adjective would have indicated a very particular gradation in skin color, the descriptor a legacy of the slave market, like the attempts to parse the exact fraction of Lucy Murphy's African American ancestry. These were words that only made sense because they had been used for generations in a vocabulary that rendered people as commodities to be sold. When Murphy's achievements made the papers, they had to be fit into that legacy for white readers, made legible and comfortable. The words had to nullify any threat he posed, not describe a man whose existence demanded that there be new vocabularies or new understandings.

The money came up often. The *New York Sportsman* pegged Murphy's 1885 wealth at between thirty and forty thousand dollars.[65] By 1886, the *Chicago Inter Ocean* claimed he was worth fifty thousand dollars, and the *San Francisco Examiner* topped them by valuing his fortune at seventy five thousand (about twenty-three million today).[66] The *Chicago Tribune* agreed with the higher figure.[67] The news even made it across the Atlantic, where British papers reported his salary as twelve thousand dollars a year.[68] The sheer size of the sums, even if there was some disagreement about just what those sums were, was the real news. But the money was often only part of a discussion of what Murphy spent it on.

The *New York Times* gave front-page coverage to the new house the Murphys bought in 1887, noting that they had paid ten thousand dollars for "a fine suburban residence."[69] Other papers followed, both in the United States and abroad.[70] Murphy led "a regular life, saving and investing his money," the press reported approvingly.[71] It made national news when he officially employed a valet (common enough for a jockey trying to keep riding gear, train tickets, and personal effects in order on the road), but he dressed with stolid conservatism.[72]

Newspapers never tired of reporting how quiet and honest he was. Sometimes that meant a thoughtful defense of his work when inevitable questions arose about how well he'd ridden or what exactly he'd said in a stewards' inquiry. "Isaac Murphy has been for many years regarded as one of our model jockeys," observed the *New York Sportsman* in one of those cases. "His opportunities to be crooked, if he were disposed to be so, have been as great, if not greater, than any rider we have ever had, and never has there been a breath of suspicion attached to his conduct. It is more than unfair to make him the object of uncalled for criticism."[73] These were the responses of knowledgeable fans and writers, lauding a professional's commitment to his craft—the kind of praise an athlete can appreciate. But newspapers tended to go beyond those assessments. He wasn't just taciturn and scrupulous: he "never made a bet in his life. He never drinks intoxicating liquor, does not swear and never tells a lie."[74] Murphy was a grown man who worked where fatal disaster could strike without warning. That kind of pattern card perfection was incredibly unlikely, as the press more quietly acknowledged, without noting the discrepancy, when they recounted his convivial evenings with his wife and friends, "smoking cigarettes, sipping wine and chatting about the many races he has won and lost."[75]

The point wasn't to establish whether Murphy actually drank, smoked, or swore. The point was to signal consistently that he was respectable and thus good and deserving. Respectability was a more urgent and contested matter for Murphy than for his white colleagues, because for him to be deserving meant to be unthreatening. Newspapers that reported his abstemious taciturnity went even further and insisted, "He mingles very little with his own race."[76] Anyone who read the racing news reasonably attentively would know that was untrue. Murphy's associations with other Black horsemen were a matter of public record, and the papers also often noted when he stayed with friends on the road, like Henry Bridgewater of St. Louis, whom the local paper called "the colored sport."[77] But, again, the point wasn't truth. The point was to insist that Murphy's success did not have any implications for other Black people, that he wouldn't want it to.

Turf chronicler John H. Davis, remembering his childhood as a racing fan, wrote, "From one end of the country to the other, he was famous, and every little boy who took any interest in racing knew of and had an admiration for Isaac Murphy." Murphy was one of the first Black athletes that white children wanted to emulate. But Davis immediately followed his recollection up: "He was black of skin, but his heart was as white as snow."[78] It was safe to admire Murphy, because somehow he wasn't truly Black. Eli Jordan himself used the same formulation: "I know the boy well, and though his skin is colored, his heart is as white as any heart could be."[79]

It was one thing for a white man to make that kind of distinction between skin and heart. It was another for the Black man who, by all accounts, was the closest thing to a father Murphy had to do the same. To say that Murphy had a white heart was to say that he deserved to reap the admiration his accolades had earned, even if Black people in general did not. The alternative was to claim that all people were entitled to equality. It's easy enough to see why a white fan might excuse his childhood affections with this kind of distinction, why he might explain to himself that admiring a Black man didn't fundamentally undermine basic tenets of racism. But to hear the same words out of Eli Jordan's mouth is to hear just how frightening it would have been to be the man whose existence seemed potentially poised to raise seismic questions. If Murphy's life somehow made a universal claim, he wouldn't be safe. And Jordan, who used to say that Murphy was the thing he was most proud of in the world, wanted him to be safe.[80]

To suggest a Black man could be a hero was an inherently political act. And so the press sometimes scoffingly assured its readers that Murphy was entirely apolitical. Tom Ochiltree, who was a former Texas Confederate and prominent horseman, liked to joke that "Murphy would be Senator from Kentucky," if the two sitting Senators, Joseph Blackburn and James Beck, had their way.[81] The joke illustrated Murphy's fame, but it depended on the very idea of him in the U.S. Senate as ridiculous. "There's Ike Murphy," reported the *Topeka Lance,* "a sinewy bit of colored humanity with a woolly head, thin withers and spurred heels, who probably never read the civil rights bill and doesn't care . . . for its contents."[82] That was double-edged strategy in a sentence: Murphy was safe because he wasn't interested in Black equality, and, in any case, he couldn't transcend his race. His physical body established everything about him as inferior. If it became too uncomfortable to see him as an exception, the experiment could be summarily abandoned. J. B. Haggin's business partner, Senator George Hearst, opined, "The negro . . . is naturally a horseman. Put him astride a horse, and in riding a race he doesn't know what fear is."[83] Murphy's success could, in the end, be put down to raw ability that owed nothing to skill or thought; he happened to benefit from one of the immutable characteristics of biological race. He proved its power as a system of organizing the world, rather than calling it into question.

This one-two punch approach, which kept Murphy's meaning carefully contained, was common in popular culture at the time. Men like Murphy and some of his athletic peers, like Peter Jackson, could be marked as different. They could make claims to re-

FREELAND.
BY LONGFELLOW, DAM BELLE KNIGHT, BY KNIGHTWOOD.

Currier and Ives print of Murphy and Freeland, 1885.
Prints and Photographs Division, Library of Congress, LC-DIG-pga-08723.

spectability and skill that in certain circumstances elevated them beyond reflexive forms of bigotry. When John L. Sullivan refused to fight Jackson because of his color, some commentators accepted his decision, but others mocked him: a real champion competed against the best and didn't find excuses to avoid them. Jackson was a man of color, "but it is equally true that so far as the qualities which go to make a man [are] concerned, Peter has somewhat the advantage of John L."[84] Elite athletes were sportsmen to be treated with respect for their prowess within the confines of their professions, and to denigrate them or refuse to face them was to mark oneself a coward.[85] These were the men who appeared alongside white athletes on cigarette and trading cards. Murphy would appear in multiple sets over the years.[86] They were the men who appeared on middle-class walls in the prints of Currier and Ives. Murphy and Freeland had their own print, and he appeared in composites of the great riders and racers of the time as well.[87]

But Currier and Ives also printed hundreds of images in their Darktown series, which by the mid-1880s supplied about a third of the firm's sales. Darktown prints depicted African Americans doing ordinary things—serving as firefighters, debating politics, riding in races—activities that the printmakers regularly mined for sentimental or heroic images in the rest of their catalog. But, unlike in the prints of Isaac Murphy, every resident of Darktown had the caricatured features popular in minstrel show blackface characters. And they failed ludicrously in every endeavor. In the racing images, riders flopped in the saddle, fell off, and otherwise demonstrated an utter incompetence intended to be comic. Darktown was the home of "coons," an increasingly popular and specific slur intended to brand Black men as hopelessly venal—too flamboyant, too violent, too hopelessly degenerate and dull to claim respect, let alone full citizenship. Darktown was a fictional place, but it served a real purpose: to offer images of a world in which white supremacy was natural and inevitable, completely impossible to challenge.[88] And Darktown was the rule, rather than the exception, in popular culture steeped in the 1880s in tales of happily enslaved people on picturesque plantations, in minstrel songs and comedy routines. These themes and assumptions reassured white people, both Northern and Southern. To admire a few particular men, to let your kids root for them, was safe precisely because they were either extraordinary or biologically ordained for inferiority.[89]

This uneasy equipoise was the place men like Murphy lived,

A CORINTHIAN RACE.
A High Toned Start.

One of several Currier and Ives Darktown prints that ridiculed
African American horsemen. Prints and Photographs Division,
Library of Congress, LC-DIG-pga-04772.

somewhere between exceptional and inferior and, either way,
doomed to prove that white people's rhetoric about race was
somehow true. But Murphy's position was even more compli-
cated because he wasn't alone. Unquestionably the preeminent
African American jockey of his time and always rated as one of the
best of all, he was never the only rider of color. The papers regularly reported the dominance of jockeys like Tony Hamilton, Pike
Barnes, Willie Simms, and George Anderson. Enough Black jockeys rode at the top level to spread the honors around at top-class
meets.[90] Sometimes comparisons to Murphy elevated another
jockey, like Pike Barnes, about ten years his junior. Barnes once
outdueled the champion in a close finish, and Murphy supposedly recommended that E. J. Baldwin hire him as his lightweight

jockey. Barnes rode for years for Baldwin at the weights Murphy couldn't manage and by the late 1880s had more than five hundred mounts a year, winning at a clip of about 35 percent.[91] In 1888, he won the first running of the Futurity, then the richest race in America, with Proctor Knott, earning commendations for brilliance and comparisons to Murphy.[92]

But Murphy wasn't always used as a shorthand for approval; he could also serve as a yardstick to judge his colleagues inadequate. He was, after all, the *Brooklyn Eagle* advised its readers, "what used to be known in the South as 'one of the house darkies.'"[93] As Northern city dwellers experimented with using the language and assumptions of slavery to describe their understandings of race, they seized on this distinction. Again, his success was turned around to prove that success wasn't what men like him were meant for. Murphy was most often held up as superior to his friend Anthony Hamilton, who usually rode at the New York tracks. Originally from South Carolina, Hamilton started as a stableboy in Charleston and then moved north to work for the trainer and jockey-maker Billy Lakeland. He rode for the most prestigious of stables, including those of J. B. Haggin, James R. Keene, George Hearst, and August Belmont.[94] Hamilton, Murphy, and their wives could often be seen at the races together. Hamilton's very dark coloring was often contrasted to Murphy's appearance. Murphy was "exceptionally intelligent looking," while Hamilton "has little breath or brain to spare." He was "uncultured and densely ignorant," a triumph of "bone over brain," "so dull he never senses danger."[95] Hamilton was posed as Murphy's foil, a living Darktown caricature.

Isaac Murphy as one man had particular meanings and burdens; Isaac Murphy as the man who represented a whole community of Black men had an even heavier load to carry. Newspapers across the country in the 1880s reprinted a complaint about his eating in a New York hotel dining room in an integrated party. This was a hotel where "he could not have bought a meal or a bed," and yet in his case "the color line seemed to be entirely washed out," the story whined.[96] We know that Murphy did attend social occasions like that and was probably often the only Black man in a convivial group, and that must have had its own perhaps accustomed but never comfortable tensions. But we don't know if this particular story is true. Even if the writer was told the Black man he complained about was Isaac Murphy, we don't know if it actually was. Murphy was a stand-in for all the Black men who might show up in segregated spaces and erode the color line, the mountain Frederick Douglass had described, until it could be washed away.

Murphy never talked publicly about how he felt about his position, what it was like to be so closely scrutinized, how tiring it was to mean so many disparate things. But it must have been another exhausting burden on top of the physical demands of his job, and those he was never reticent about. So it is not surprising that, by the end of the 1880s, he was thinking about a new direction for his career. Rumor had it that Mike and Phil Dwyer, the Brooklyn meatpacking magnates who had owned Miss Woodford, were supposedly disenchanted with their longtime jockey, Jimmy McLaughlin. A contract for Murphy seemed to be in the offing.[97] It never quite materialized, but Murphy did start riding often for the brothers, balancing his commitments to them with his contract with Baldwin. He now spent more and more time at the New York tracks, riding some of the great stars of the Dwyer stable, like Hanover and Kingston. After August, he hopped from track to track in New York and New Jersey, going from Saratoga to Coney Island to Brooklyn to Morris Park for weeks, picking up rides not only from Baldwin and the Dwyers but from other New

York owners.[98] He had always spent some of the end of the season on the New York circuit, but now he stayed longer, and he altered the seasonal rounds that had dictated his life for a decade. Now he might go to New York in the spring and summer, riding in the East instead of at meetings closer to home, where he had cut his teeth.[99] Sometimes he now even left Chicago, site of his greatest triumphs, for New York, as he did in July of 1889, when he hopped a midnight train to ride J. B. Haggin's two-year-old star Salvator at Monmouth Park.[100] By the spring of 1890, the rumor was that Murphy would ride almost exclusively in the East, a mark of his status at the pinnacle of his profession.[101] He may have been banking as much prestige and cash as he could, knowing that the situation was unsustainable. Repeatedly, he announced that he would not lose weight to take rides anymore. Though the weights in England were as much as ten pounds heavier, even that higher scale had "proved little better than murder to jockeys" like Fred Archer.[102] Repeatedly, he announced he would retire.[103]

And then in mid-summer 1887, Edward West, his younger colleague in the Baldwin stable, was killed in a chaotic two-year-old race at Saratoga.[104] West sustained a brain injury that paralyzed half of his body and died several days after the accident.[105] Only a couple of years Murphy's junior, West was from Louisville. They had known each other since they had both ridden for Ed Corrigan.[106] Murphy helped John West gather his son's possessions and the salary he had due and get the body shipped back to Kentucky for burial. The papers announced that Baldwin would be taking on West's younger brother as a jockey. The kid was sixteen and supposedly weighed sixty-five pounds.[107]

Jockeys can't think about the dangers of their job, because they couldn't keep riding if they did. When they list the bones they've broken or recall an accident, the click of distancing mechanisms is audible. So Murphy wouldn't necessarily have thought about his own mortality any more than usual as he comforted John West. But a man who was about his own age, who was from around his own home, who had followed almost the same professional path he had, was dead. And here was his brother, tiny and frail, ready to walk that same path. It was a visceral reminder that his professional life would almost inevitably be a fleeting one. Too much pain, too much danger, too many boys who were young and malleable and light.

Murphy knew exactly what he planned to do next. Many jockeys took a stab at the next step up in a stable hierarchy—training. The skills necessary to being a good jockey weren't the same as those of a good trainer, but Murphy had worked around good trainers all his professional life. He knew horses, and he had connections.[108] He and John T. Clay were the kind of friends who are more like family. Clay had trained the great Himyar and bought the filly Jewell Ban from his employer, Barack G. Thomas of Dixiana Farm in Lexington. Murphy got a close view of Jewell Ban in Lexington's Ashland Oaks, when Clay, knowing his old friend's tactics, told his jockey to keep her beside Murphy's mount, toward the rear of the field. He knew she had the speed to beat whatever Murphy's horse kept in reserve, and "sure enough, Jewell Ban burned up that last furlong."[109] The big chestnut filly went on to win the Kentucky Oaks, making John T. Clay the only African American yet to own an Oaks winner.[110]

But no one was better than Edward Brown, Murphy's friend and neighbor, at fostering a young horse's talent. Ben Brush, the nondescript two-year-old that Brown turned into an unbeaten champion, went on to win the Kentucky Derby of 1896 for Mike Dwyer, to whom Brown had sold the colt for what would now be more than half a million dollars.[111] Brown would repeat the magic trick when he sold Plaudit as a two-year-old to John E. Madden, then embarking on a legendary bloodstock career, and saw the colt go on to win the 1898 Kentucky Derby. The African American exercise rider Marshall Lilly had his first racetrack job with Brown when he was a teenager and galloped Plaudit. He saw all the high rollers of the early twentieth century, but he always remembered the wad of cash his first boss carried around.[112]

At the track near his house, Murphy could see Brown, Clay, and his neighbor Abe Perry working horses.[113] He began filling the barn on his property, planning to be back on the rail in the early mornings, this time giving instructions.[114] He registered his colors, identifying himself as the owner of a stable. His jockeys would wear a black jacket, white belt, and red cap with a green tassel. He would ride his own horses, though not when one belonging to E. J. Baldwin was running. Though ultimately he planned to train them himself, he was still an active jockey, so the horses were in the care of friends like Charles Anderson, a Lexington trainer.[115] William Walker, who had moved on to his own second career as a bloodstock consultant, bought a two-year-old named Barrister and then sold him to Murphy, both of them probably hoping to make the horse into something and turn a profit.[116] Murphy backed up his opinion of Pike Barnes by giving him the mount on Barrister as a three-year-old, and the horse won at Lexington and established himself as a potential Kentucky Derby starter. Murphy was riding in New York that week, but it must have seemed a portent of things to come; he might be a jockey in New York, but at home he was an owner and trainer, mentoring other jockeys and looking to a long career.[117] Barrister didn't quite shape into a Derby colt, but he ran well at Louisville, St. Louis, and Chicago that spring and summer, well enough for Murphy to sell him to the veteran horseman Green B. Morris for four thousand dollars, a fancy price for a horse who had been shuffled out of his first stable.[118] Murphy also tapped his roots as he built his string, buying Fabulous, by Longfellow and out of a Falsetto half-sister, from

Fleetwood Farm. He also bought a half-brother to Falsetto himself. These were horses Eli Jordan had known from their babyhood, and they were relatives of some of his greatest mounts. Murphy had enough confidence to nominate Fabulous for the American Derby.[119] Some of his stable remained in Lucy Murphy's name, probably to avoid official conflicts of interest, and Murphy also took stakes in horses in exchange for negotiating their sale.[120] In other words, he operated like a horseman who planned to make his living by his expertise, since his wits would last much longer than his weight.

But he wasn't quite ready to stop riding. After all, he'd ridden the highest percentage of winners in America multiple times in the 1880s, even though he curated his book of mounts carefully.[121] But getting back in riding shape, never easy, was harder than ever. In February 1890, he weighed 145 pounds; in weeks, he would have to be thirty pounds lighter. So he delayed. In earlier years, he had a standing contract, signed months in advance. This year, he and Baldwin had let their contract lapse, and he had still made no official commitments as spring racing began.[122] But he made exceptions for old friends. He rode Outbound for Fleetwood and Eli Jordan at his home track in Lexington in May and earned a rousing ovation from the crowd, pleased to see him back in the saddle for the first time that year.[123] And he agreed to ride for Ed Corrigan again, taking the mount on the highly regarded Riley in the Kentucky Derby.[124] Riley was a strapping bay son of Longfellow, out of a War Dance mare, already battle-hardened after six wins and twelve starts as a two-year-old.[125]

Murphy hadn't had the mount before and didn't try to get on him before the Derby. He went to the barns at Churchill Downs to pick up his colors on Derby Day and told the grooms he didn't need to see the horse: "I would see him when I came to ride him."

When Riley took the track, the crowd cheered him and Murphy, but Murphy didn't take a ceremonial gallop past the stand. Instead, he took his horse straight to the start. "I wanted to get to the post and have the race over. I was not feeling very well, not having eaten anything all day." The Derby demanded that Riley carry 118 pounds, so Murphy had managed, once again, to take the weight off quickly. He let Riley settle toward the back as the speed horses wore each other out. Then he surged forward. Riley tried to swerve, but Murphy kept him doing his job, and the horse won by lengths, with Murphy riding hands and heels.[126] Murphy had come for one ride, not to compete for the whole meet, but Corrigan came to Murphy's house to ask him to return and ride Riley in the Clark Stakes, usually the follow-up contest for Derby winners in those days. Murphy agreed and rode Riley to victory again.[127]

After his second Kentucky Derby win, Murphy left home to head east. After months of uncertainty, he had signed a contract, this time to ride for J. B. Haggin. Reportedly, Murphy would receive fifteen thousand dollars a year, equivalent to about four million today. It may have seemed the perfect short-term deal for an athlete in the twilight of his career. It was more money than he had ever had in salary, and other riders would tackle the mounts on younger horses that demanded lower weights. Murphy would be primarily responsible for Haggin's two superstars, Salvator and Firenze.[128]

Murphy boarded at the Osborn House, a favored stopping place for horsemen and fans during the New York racing season, at the intersection of Jay and Willoughby, in the heart of downtown Brooklyn.[129] From there he could commute to all the local racetracks, which were bunched together near the shore, or hop a train to Saratoga. Trains also ran directly to the Sheepshead Bay racetrack, where he would pull off his first overwhelming success of the summer. The Suburban Handicap was a relatively new race in those days, but it already carried a big reputation. The Suburban of 1890 drew the "best horses in training, and they rank with the best that have ever worn plates."[130] A record crowd, including politicians, bankers, actors, and babies, turned out. The New York City Board of Aldermen couldn't manage a quorum, because they were all at the Suburban.[131] Ninety-one bookmakers plied their trade in a 300,000-square-foot enclosure, packed down to the square inch.[132] They made Murphy's mount the favorite.

Salvator had established himself as a good horse when he finished third in the Futurity as a two-year-old. His sire, Prince Charlie, had won the 2,000 Guineas, the first leg of the English Triple Crown, and his dam, Salina, had been a tough racehorse.[133] Salvator, a big, muscular chestnut, took after his sire, moving with a lordly air, like "a prince among horses."[134] As a three-year-old, he captured some of the big stakes of the East.[135] Going into his four-year-old campaign in 1890, he bid fair to be one of the best horses in training.[136] Insiders plunked their money down on him for the Suburban, while others looked at Tenny's four straight victories and sided with him, so the two went to the post essentially joint favorites.[137]

Fred Taral, one of the great jockeys of the time, went to the front on Cassius, hoping to steal an insurmountable lead, since Salvator was giving his mount twenty pounds in handicap weight. But Murphy kept the chestnut within striking distance. As they entered the last half mile, Tenny threatened to take the lead on the outside, and the crowd roared, only to gasp as Murphy came creeping up to Cassius and passed him, "riding as though the animal were some cunningly-devised mechanism, whose limitations have long since been ascertained and who can be sent forward or backward to the fractional part of an inch whenever the operator so wills it." Salvator was truly the "quadruped wonder of the age," raved the *Brooklyn Eagle*.[138] The crowd carried Murphy from the judges' stand to the jockeys' room in a giant floral horseshoe, acclaiming him yet again as "the best 'jock' in the country."[139]

Tenny's owner immediately announced that he believed his horse had been the victim of bad racing luck. He challenged J. B. Haggin to match Salvator with Tenny, and the Coney Island Jockey Club agreed to host the race at Sheepshead Bay, with each contestant putting up twenty-five hundred dollars and the club matching them to make a total purse of ten thousand dollars.[140] As the appointed date of June 25 approached, the contest was "the chief topic of conversation among racing men."[141] Fans savored the matchup not only between the two great horses but between the two jockeys, whose styles contrasted so sharply: Murphy was the canny, meticulous judge of how to ease a horse to victory, while his rival "Snapper" Garrison was the hustling finisher par excellence.[142]

The crowds, "thousands of men who worked indoors and out," women, and children, streamed into the track on the day.[143] As the horses went to the post, fans shouted and hooted; Garrison responded, but Murphy remained silent. As he and Salvator cantered to the start together, they "looked the idealization of horse and jockey . . . and round after round of applause came from the masses of people in the stand, on the lawn, and, in fact, every place where any sight of the race could be gained."[144] For the first quarter mile the two horses ran together. Murphy didn't seem to move, but Salvator gained inch by inch, until he was more than a length ahead. The tempo increased, until men began to gape at their watches, sure they were seeing things. With a furlong to go, Salvator was two lengths in front, but Tenny slowly, impossibly, began to gain.[145] "Then came a time when people held their breath, when they live[d] only in the eye and ear," as the result hung in the balance. Garrison threw Tenny at the wire, but Salvator won by a short head.[146] He had equaled records for the fractions and

The finish of the match race between Salvator and Tenny, 1890.
Salvator and Murphy are on the rail. Keeneland Library Hemment Collection.

shattered the record for a mile and a quarter by more than a second, finishing in 2:05.[147] (Kentucky Derby and Preakness winner Spectacular Bid set the present record of 1:57 4/5 in 1980, but he had the advantage of modern technology in shoeing and surface.) John Hemment, the track photographer, caught the finish with a lens that worked in thousandths of a second and documented how close it was.[148] Everyone went home, *Turf, Field and Farm* reflected, "thoroughly convinced that he had witnessed something that would do to tell in after years to his children and grandchildren."[149] The turf writer John Hervey, who lived to watch Man o' War, always staunchly insisted that Salvator was the greatest racehorse he had ever seen.[150]

Murphy had been at the top of his profession for a decade by then, but those few weeks of summer 1890 were magical. Though eighteen horses had entered the Monmouth Cup, no one cared to take Salvator on, and he and Murphy galloped to victory in solitary splendor.[151] The second largest crowd in the history of Monmouth Park turned up to see Salvator once again battle Tenny, this time at a mile and a half in the Senior Champion Stakes. More than forty other entries had melted away to leave them alone. This time Salvator made the pace, with Tenny close behind, until they turned for home, when Garrison brought his horse up to challenge and pulled level with the leader. Murphy then let Salvator out a notch, and the big chestnut soared home by several lengths.[152]

That same day, Murphy scored again, in the Junior Champion Stakes for two-year-olds. Nineteen of the best juveniles in training answered the call to the post, the lineup stretching from one rail of the track to the other. Green B. Morris's Strathmeath was an experienced runner but was only fourth-favorite behind more glamorous contenders. Morris had booked Murphy, hoping his acute judgment would help the colt in such a huge field. Murphy kept the gelding behind the leaders, waiting for his chance. As they reached the wire, Strathmeath came "with a rush like a rocket" and passed the leader to win by a vanishingly small margin.[153] The two victories together, within minutes of each other, tapped gushers of praise. The Brooklyn papers reminded their readers that Salvator "has . . . the inestimable privilege of being ridden by the best jockey of the day. . . . He is the Archer of his time."[154] Of course Murphy was grinning as he returned to the paddock; the day "was the supreme climax of a grand career."[155]

The Salvator Club, a loosely organized group of socially and politically prominent men from the New York area, had dubbed themselves with the champion's name in honor of the money they'd won on him that summer. After the Senior Champion, they celebrated together at an immense clambake under the trees near Monmouth Park. The papers reported that "the champagne ran in streams and rivers," and "half the judicial and political 'somebodies' of New York were present." Judges, mayors, and police commissioners ate, drank, sang, and applauded as Murphy was presented with a silver-mounted whip in recognition of his achievements. The theatrical star DeWolf Hopper recited his famous version of "Casey at the Bat."[156]

Murphy's glorious match race victory had drawn attention in other circles as well. T. Thomas Fortune had been born enslaved in the Florida Panhandle and forged a career in journalism; by 1890, he had founded the *New York Globe*, which became the *New York Freeman* and then the *New York Age*, the most widely circulated African American paper of the time.[157] Fortune used his editorial pen to call attention to national problems affecting people of color. He focused on protecting African Americans from lynching and mob violence, fighting voter suppression, demanding equal access to education, reforming prison systems that used convict labor, and securing equal access to public facilities.[158] The breadth of those issues reflected Fortune's ability to identify the common roots and multiple branches of racism. Throughout the 1880s, with the support of some of the most prominent Black leaders of his time, Fortune advocated for a national organization—along the lines the NAACP would later take—to tackle these problems.

Booker T. Washington called for chapters in every town and charged Black Americans to "push the battle to the gate."[159] By the early months of 1890, dozens of local and state chapters had been formed to combat multiple manifestations of racism and had convened to discuss their ongoing strategy.[160]

Around the same time, Fortune staged a personal protest with the assistance of his friend and attorney T. McCants Stewart, who had been born in South Carolina and remained active in civil rights causes when he moved to New York.[161] Fortune entered the Trainor Hotel on 33rd Street in June 1890 and ordered a beer; the waiter and then the proprietor refused to serve him, and Fortune refused to leave until they did. The police arrested him for disorderly conduct. The charges were dropped, but Fortune sued the owner of the hotel for ten thousand dollars. The chapters of Fortune's league mobilized public sentiment in support of the suit, and Stewart, in a powerful closing statement to the court, reminded the all-white jury of the provisions of the Fourteenth Amendment and the right of African Americans "to every civil and political right guaranteed . . . by the Constitution and the law of the land." Washington, who was in the courtroom, hurried to shake his hand. The jury ultimately awarded Fortune damages and a thousand dollars.[162]

Fortune saw himself as part of a rising generation of what he proudly called "Afro-American agitators," a term he borrowed from the Atlanta editor and civic booster Henry Grady, who envisioned an amicable partnership between white Northerners and Southerners. Grady believed America should be ruled by businessmen, with laborers and people of color a permanent working class, to be kept repressed by rhetoric and occasionally by violence. So when he spoke of "Afro-American agitators," he was offering a mocking condemnation, but Fortune adopted the epithet as a *nom de guerre*.[163] "There must be as to citizenship," he insisted, "absolute equality, or the letter and the spirit of the Constitution become nullities, and republican government an experiment and not a reality."[164]

Fortune had an expansive view of activism. As he said at the national meeting of his civil rights organization in early 1890, "Revolutions are of many sorts." Some of them were obvious, but others could be subtle.[165] Fortune saw revolutionary potential in African American jockeys. They won in open competition, and their success gave activists an example to point to.[166] Examples like Murphy could, Fortune hoped, "make men lose, in measure, whatever they may possess of color prejudice."[167]

As Fortune and Stewart pursued their antidiscrimination suit that summer, they went together to see the Salvator-Tenny match race. Fortune admitted he didn't frequent the track, and Stewart hadn't been since he was a boy. But they noticed how many Black people were there. A friend introduced them to Murphy after the race. Fortune couldn't help himself and had to ask. Did Murphy really like close finishes, as people speculated? Murphy looked him in the eye, smiled, and said four words. "I ride to win." It was the answer of a man sure of his powers and determined to succeed, the kind of man who not only clearly deserved equality, but could inspire others to demand it.[168]

CHAPTER 4

———

"The Wrong This Day Done"

URPHY'S GREATEST EXPLOITS in the summer of 1890 were his victories with Salvator, but he also partnered Firenze, the other Haggin stable superstar. Haggin bought her as a yearling, and she began winning at two and never stopped. Delicate and quick-striding, she seemed sweet and quiet but could kick like a showgirl when she felt like it, her trainer reported.[1] Jimmy McLaughlin, who rode her, as he had ridden Miss Woodford, gave Firenze a slight edge over the other mare, because she "would run all day."[2] Firenze was six in 1890, but she was still winning and placing in high-stakes competition with regular ease.[3] Murphy rode her eight times.[4] A few of those eight included major stakes performances in New York during his golden weeks that summer.[5]

The Monmouth Handicap seemed tailor-made for the great jockey and the great mare: she went off 6 to 5.[6] As usual, Murphy seemed to be trying to hold up his mount and let others make the running, but she kept shooting into the lead and then falling back. By the time they reached the top of the stretch he looked to be clinging to her mouth for balance. As she passed the finish line in last place, she swerved toward the fence, and the crowd yelled in horror. He managed to stop her but then fell out of the saddle. An assistant starter caught the horse and helped him back aboard, while the crowd gaped and gasped. In the paddock, Murphy dismounted without officially getting clearance from racing officials, breaking a rule he had been following for fifteen years. He seemed disoriented.[7]

What had happened? The officials at Monmouth immediately started an investigation. David D. Withers, who reigned over Monmouth, had worked his way up in a New York trading firm and represented them in New Orleans before he struck out on his own as a cotton broker. Withers was thus a representative of the antebellum history of the turf, the decades when enslaved men had ridden in New Orleans, when fortunes were made from the crops grown by their friends and relatives. He had been one of many prominent Confederate sympathizers who had moved back to New York after the war, where he had been welcomed for his long racing experience and the imprimatur of planter power he brought with him.[8] Withers chaired the investigation committee, and Murphy drove over from the home where he and Lucy were staying in the resort town of Red Bank for the hearing.[9]

Murphy was adamant that, despite speculation to the contrary, he had not been drunk. He had been preparing to ride at 118 pounds, ten pounds lower than Firenze had carried, for another mount. And he had planned to ride Salvator in a special attempt to break the record for a mile, which meant reducing his weight to 110 pounds, punishingly low for him at this point in his career. Rather than eating breakfast the morning of the race, he had drunk a few milk punches before leaving home. Nineteenth-century medicine sometimes vaguely attributed stimulant properties to the combination of alcohol and dairy products. When he arrived at the track, he and Lucy sat together in the stands, and he drank

Apollinaris mineral water and ginger ale. Apollinaris was brand-name imported water; doctors endorsed its healthful and invigorating properties.[10] (One of them was J. Marion Sims, who had pioneered gynecology by experimenting on the bodies of enslaved women.) Murphy had been fine when he got in the saddle, but the exertion of the race was too much. He painted himself as a victim of the demands of his profession, desperately trying to summon up the energy to compete as he starved his body, and his judges believed him. Track staff, Murphy's valet (whom the newspapers always reminded their readers was white), and Firenze's trainer Matt Byrnes all corroborated his account. Even David Pulsifer, Tenny's owner, who had no particular reason to do Murphy any favors, said he figured that the combination of liquids on an empty stomach followed by intense physical activity could cause crippling vertigo. The authorities rejected the argument that Murphy had tentatively advanced that he might have been drugged, possibly to try to affect the outcome of the race, on which hundreds of thousands of dollars had been bet.[11]

The question of Murphy's sobriety wasn't entirely new. While newspapers had depicted him as either completely abstemious or scrupulously careful in his drinking, they also sometimes reported episodes where he seemed to be slightly inebriated. Occasionally, he seemed more talkative or more unsteady than usual, enough to provoke comment for a man so conspicuously and consistently in control of his body, attuned as he was by profession and by the codes of racial hierarchy to constant self-scrutiny.[12] But they almost universally dismissed the episodes and defended him. Everyone knew, insisted the *Louisville Courier Journal*, that he only drank for medicinal, professional purposes; he shouldn't be stigmatized for using alcohol that way. Jockeys drank champagne because it was regarded as a stimulant, mild nutritional supplement, and nausea remedy.[13] This use of champagne is perhaps less archaic than it seems. Steve Cauthen, who rode Affirmed to the Triple Crown in 1978 at the age of eighteen and went on to dominate British racing, used champagne as a substitute for food and a mood enhancer.[14] If that was what Murphy was doing, men in his profession were still doing it a century later.

The racing authorities seem to have decided that Murphy's condition was ultimately due to his weight loss regimen. But they also appear to have decided that since he had, after all, drunk alcohol on the morning of the race and since he had lost a major stakes contest in such conspicuous fashion on such a heavy favorite, they were obliged to discipline him. They suspended him for two race meetings. The blow was a bitter one, particularly for a man whose respectability and reliability were such a proudly professed part of his reputation. The suspension also meant that Murphy could not ride Salvator in his speed test on the new straight track at Monmouth Park. Matt Byrnes still complained years later that, though the horse set a new record at 1:35½, Murphy's judgment of pace and familiarity with Salvator would have shaved a couple of seconds off the time. And Murphy himself must have been profoundly disappointed not to partner the great stallion in the final test of his wonderful summer.[15] Meanwhile, "Snapper" Garrison and Marty Bergen rode Firenze to significant victories.[16]

Even worse, the press abruptly stopped excusing Murphy's alcohol use. Their main message was shrill and constant: Murphy was a disgraceful, disgusting drunk. Occasionally they acknowledged other potential explanations for his behavior but only as an afterthought. Suddenly reporters assured their readers that it was widely known of Murphy that, "The champagne bottle has been his god, and there is probably no man in clubdom in New York to-day that can punish as much of the sparkling fluid as Murphy."[17] J. B. Haggin should fire him immediately. "How he can tolerate a further connection of such a person . . . is difficult to see."[18] He was lucky no one had physically attacked him at the track, since "it looked at one time as if the crowd would beat the life out of him. If someone had . . . given him a sound thrashing, nobody would have interfered."[19] He had inconvenienced and angered fans; surely they had the right to hurt him.

Some of the ugliest stories attributed the episode at Monmouth to the Salvator Club party, where "there was champagne galore—rivers of it."[20] How he could still have been drunk days after the celebration seemed difficult to explain, but, as the *New York Times* direly insisted, the party had "laid the foundations" for his behavior.[21] The vague language suggests that the newspapers were trying to articulate a more amorphous sense of wrongness for which they were punishing the jockey. It wasn't necessarily the champagne. It was the party itself, all those powerful white men not just applauding Murphy but sitting down to eat with him, having their photos taken with him in dress clothes.

Some fans and reporters complained that the summer of 1890 had been an unprecedented showcase for Black success across sports, as Peter Jackson defeated white opponents in the ring and Murphy won repeatedly on Salvator. Those victories had visible consequences, like the Salvator Club bash that Murphy had attended. Peter Jackson had started acting "as if he had actually come into possession of his ancestral dominions on the Congo."[22] What if Black athletes were no longer grateful or taciturn? What if their very success called into question the supposed verities of racial hierarchy and inspired demands for change, as T. Thomas Fortune and his allies hoped? Men who raised those questions were dangerous. And Murphy was raising them on the front page of the biggest Black newspaper in America. Whether white reporters had seen Fortune's stories or not, they could see the same possibilities he saw.

Those possibilities seemed to loom even larger that summer because of what was happening off the track. In Washington, the Federal Elections Bill, sponsored by Henry Cabot Lodge of Massachusetts, would allow for federal supervision of a congressional election if a nominal number of citizens in an area requested it, a policy that might frustrate Southern attempts to suppress Black votes. Even as the bill foundered in the Senate, white Southerners raged and feared.[23] "Probably Mr. Murphy doesn't care whether the Federal Election bill passes or not," one newspaper gratuitously informed its readers in its coverage of the Monmouth investigation.[24] Jamming in mention of it suggested that Murphy somehow seemed connected to the bill, even if he never opened his mouth on the subject. He and it both offered a potential future of full Black citizenship. And so readers were assured that he really didn't—and, in any case, he could be punished for it.

That fall, Murphy got the mount on Firenze back and rode her to a very creditable second to Raceland, a worthy foe who had beaten her before. The crowd applauded his return when he came out on the track.[25] But the effects of the day at Monmouth clearly lingered. Stories trickled out about multiple doctors working for weeks, trying to stop his vomiting and stomach pain.[26] That winter he went through a bout of pneumonia. He stayed in bed and wrapped his stomach in flannel bandages. People talked about how drawn his face looked and wondered if he was going to die. Sometimes they speculated that he had truly been drugged at Monmouth and was still wracked by some toxin in his system; other times they simply acknowledged that his profession had compromised his health and that, as one paper put it, "his constitution has been considerably involved over the last year or two."[27]

When he was ready to get back on a horse, he stayed close to home, rebuilding his career on the trust of old friends. At the

Murphy dressed to ride at one of the New York tracks.
Keeneland Library Hemment Collection.

Lexington meeting that spring, he rode for Eli Jordan.[28] Dudley Allen, the longtime Lexington trainer, was a savvy and experienced horseman; he had worked Vagrant to win the 1876 Kentucky Derby, though J. T. Williams's name was on the official records. So he knew within minutes of looking at a group of yearlings that he wanted Kingman.[29] The horse was a bay with a white star and disproportionate jaws that gave his head an odd shape, but his gallop was low and long and ground-eating. Allen both trained him and co-owned him with white Thoroughbred enthusiast Kinzea Stone under the banner of Jacobin Stables.[30] Kingman had won or placed in good races on the Western circuit as a two-year-old, so Allen must have been pleased to get a crack at Murphy for the colt's three-year-old campaign.[31] Murphy won twice with Kingman at the Lexington meeting in the spring of 1891, including in the Phoenix Hotel Stakes, the traditional Lexington Derby prep.[32] Black bettors laid their money down heavily on the colt ridden, trained, and proudly owned by Black men when Allen took his horse to Churchill Downs for the Derby.[33]

Allen stabled Kingman in his lucky stall, where he'd kept Vagrant before the Derby, and planned. Balgowan, his horse's main opposition, would keep a falsely slow pace, tricking the others into thinking that he was going as fast as he could, when he was truly saving speed for a surprising spurt in the homestretch. Allen figured to foil that plan; besides, a slow pace favored Kingman, since Allen wasn't quite sure he could stay the distance.[34] He instructed Murphy "to walk if Balgowan walked."[35]

The 1891 Derby drew the biggest crowd in the race's history up to that time. People streamed into Churchill Downs until every space was full. When Kingman and Murphy appeared, there came a tide of "cheers that surrounding knobs and hilltops took up and echoed back again."[36] The four runners ambled for a mile, as Murphy followed instructions and waited, lurking with Balgowan in the rear. With a half mile left, the jockeys went to work, and Balgowan took the lead, with Murphy, in typical fashion, still biding his time. It wasn't until the last furlong that he sent Kingman to the lead and got him home by a length.[37]

Allen and Stone were said to have paid Murphy a thousand-dollar bonus for his victory.[38] But more importantly he had won his third Derby, a record that would stand until 1948, when Eddie Arcaro won a fourth Derby with Triple Crown winner Citation. And Murphy had won it for a Black man he had known for years, a man who had served, like his father, during the war for emancipation, who lived only a few blocks from his house. His career had been permanently altered the previous summer, but the men who had taught him his trade still respected him, and he used his skill to showcase their talents to the world.

Murphy may have had more time that winter to socialize in the community that had fostered and supported him, as he recovered from the previous year's racing. Anthony Hamilton married Annie Messley of St. Louis, and the bride and groom went from their wedding to Lexington for receptions with racetrack friends. The lavish ceremony made national news, as did the party Murphy threw for his friend.[39] The guest list included many of Lexington's Black horsemen, like John T. Clay, Edward Brown, William Walker, Tom Britton, and their families, along with friends like Leonard McPheeters, who worked at the Phoenix Hotel, and Benjamin Franklin, one of the local barbers. The Lexington papers described the ladies' dresses and the dancing and concluded, "The reception he gave has seldom been equaled even in white circles."[40]

It was a banner time for weddings among the group of friends. William Walker married Hannah Estill, a neighborhood girl, at Murphy's house that June.[41] Murphy also attended the wedding of jockey Tom Britton, scion of a prominent Lexington family of

African American professionals, that spring.[42] In 1892, Murphy's cousin got married, and this time Abe Perry and his wife hosted the reception.[43] When Isaac and Lucy Murphy renewed their own vows in January 1893, it made the local society page.[44] Weddings were to be savored for people who still remembered vividly when they and their parents, like Isaac's own, had no legal right to marriage. They were a celebration of a community determined to survive and flourish.

But weddings were not the only sign of a thriving community. Horsemen contributed to charities that assisted their neighbors.[45] They helped put on theater productions, like the performance of *Cinderella* that Abe Perry and John Clay's children acted in.[46] And they participated in the Lexington Colored Fair, an organization that put on an annual gala that showcased local livestock and handicrafts to thousands of visitors. The booths featured portraits of Frederick Douglass, T. Thomas Fortune, and other African American leaders. The fair's officers included some of Murphy's closest friends and associates, many of them leaders of Kentucky's Black community.[47]

Certainly, the conversation would have turned to politics at Murphy's parties, given the guest lists and local events. In late 1891, Kentucky joined other Southern states in proposing the legalization of segregated train transportation, and African Americans in the state mobilized to prevent the law's passage. Black access to public facilities differed across Kentucky, but the new law seemed a decisive step back down the road to full government sponsorship of racial hierarchy.[48] Surely Murphy and his colleagues, who traveled by train constantly for work, followed the debates closely.

In January 1892 hundreds of Black citizens filled the Kentucky state capitol at Frankfort to protest the bill, their ranks composed of men and women intent on preserving the hard-won gains of years.[49] They presented impassioned statements to the governor and legislature, reminding them that, "we are not ignorant of the law of the land . . . known as the fourteenth amendment . . . a constitutional guarantee that there shall be no discrimination between citizens of the United States except by due process of law."[50] Mary Britton, a prominent Lexington teacher, put her case to the legislature simply: "A law based solely upon color is unjust and un-American, as it denies that class of citizens the just and equitable recognition to which they are entitled."[51] Mary Britton had been a guest in the Murphys' house; she was Tom Britton's sister.[52] Edward Chenault had been to the same parties and played a major role in the Colored Fair and Lexington's Republican organization. He served as the county representative to the state-wide separate coach law protest group.[53] Lexington African Americans staged a boycott of white merchants who supported the law, worrying James Ware, another friend of Murphy's. Ware was a barber who depended on white customers and said he opposed the law but was concerned the protests might harm his business.[54] Murphy was surrounded by people who were deeply involved in the battle over segregation, people who saw both what they had gained and what they might lose.

Despite Black citizens' staunch efforts, the legislature enacted the separate coach law. In response, hundreds of activists attended an organizational meeting in Lexington in the summer of 1892. They framed the stakes in historical terms. They were the survivors of America Murphy Burns's generation, the grown children of Isaac Murphy's. Local leader J. C. Jackson, who had been a guest of Murphy's, traced the building of free lives after emancipation and summed up the meeting's message: "we can not now step back."[55] And that was precisely what the separate coach law threatened. Legally mandated segregation was not a minor inconvenience, yet another example of chipping away at or limiting the meaning of citizenship in daily life. It was "a crisis that will try us as by fire and call forth . . . the sturdy qualities of an enlightened manhood that enables one to contend for his rights as guaranteed by the laws of the land, even though he must contend against great odds."[56]

Evansville minister William H. Anderson and his wife sued the Louisville and Nashville Railroad for enforcing the law against them in 1893, sparking a series of legal challenges.[57] In the summer of 1894, Murphy's dear friend John T. Clay sued the L&N for expelling him from a whites-only smoking car.[58] We do not know what the two men said to each other about the case. But we do know that, as Murphy himself became a figure in debates over civil rights nationally, he had a deeply personal connection to people fighting against discrimination in his own hometown. As he thought about his future, both his opportunities and his obligations must have weighed on his mind.

In 1891 Murphy seemed to answer his critics when he placed with Tenny for David Pulsifer in the Metropolitan Handicap and won the Red Bank Stakes with a two-year-old owned by D. D. Withers himself.[59] The men who had judged him clearly continued to endorse his abilities. And suddenly a new retainer was on offer. In the summer of 1890, Frank Ehret, the son of millionaire New York brewer George Ehret, "decided to give up lawn-tennis and yachting and devote his attention, time, and money to horse-racing."[60] Frank's sister Anna, one of the dollar princesses sent to Europe to catch husbands in that period, married a German baron that summer.[61] Ehret bought out the racing stable of Theodore Winters, one of the stalwarts of the California turf and the breeder of Emperor of Norfolk.[62] And he went shopping for elite trainers and jockeys to partner his new horses. It was an ostentatious strategy, but no horseman minds ostentation too much, as long as the checks clear.

Ehret landed on Jimmy McLaughlin, Murphy's old rival, who, like Murphy, seemed to be nearing the end of his career. But McLaughlin ended his relationship with the stable in a tangle of litigation.[63] Almost immediately thereafter, Murphy took his place.[64] With Ehret's stars, like Yorkville Belle, Rey del Rey, and Demuth, Murphy rode again in the "peculiarly graceful style which made him famous," winning at the big tracks in New York.[65]

By the end of the summer of 1892, however, the relationship between Murphy and the Ehret stable had soured. Stable management complained that he wasn't living up to expectations. Murphy countered that his mounts weren't prepared to compete at the highest level, and commentators sided with him.[66] The stable initially refused to release him from his contract but also refused to mount him on their horses, so Murphy sued, retaining the services of attorney Abe Hummel.[67] Hummel was the junior partner of the formidable New York team of Howe and Hummel. They had represented P. T. Barnum and Victoria Woodhull, along with some of the city's most famous criminals.[68] Their offices, located across the street from New York's municipal jail, the Tombs, had a forty-foot sign that lit up at night and staff onsite twenty-four hours a day to assist clients, including jailbreakers who stopped there first.[69] But Hummel, who was only five feet tall and dressed meticulously in black suits and patent leather, pointed-toe shoes, skillfully combined his leisure time, in which he was an inveterate railbird and first-nighter, with his profession. He represented actors and horsemen and pioneered the enforcement of contracts in the entertainment industry.[70] Murphy went directly to a man who understood racing and the law intimately. Though Murphy didn't recoup his riding fees, he did separate himself from Ehret. Later that year, Ehret quit the track, when his father lost his taste for paying the bills.[71]

Murphy had lost a regular relationship with one employer, but he hadn't left racing by any means. Fred Taral, one of the superstars of the period, observed that Murphy could "still give any jockey in the business 'pointers' on riding races."[72] An informal poll at Churchill Downs found a majority of horsemen of the opinion that Murphy was still the best rider in the country. There were rumors that he would return to New York as the retained rider of James R. Keene or August Belmont.[73] Instead he rode freelance, often for Lexington owners, with reasonable success. When his neighbor Edward Brown decided Ducat was the best two-year-old he had in training, he retained Murphy to ride him for a fee of a thousand dollars.[74]

Murphy would have had plenty to discuss with Brown. He would now be first and foremost a trainer, he began telling people.[75] His friend John Clay probably alerted him to The Hero, a horse Clay trained to win several races as a two-year-old. Murphy bought him, hoping he could turn him into a stakes winner at three.[76] Along with The Hero, he acquired several others.[77] By the spring of 1894, the pride of his stable were two three-year-olds, Valiant and Enid, both by the young sire The Chevalier, like Salvator a son of Prince Charlie. Watching Valiant work in the mornings at Lexington, the railbirds said he would "take a lot of beating" in the Phoenix Hotel Stakes. The colt didn't win the race, which went to Chant, that year's Kentucky Derby winner, but he won stakes later that spring.[78] Murphy seemed at least reasonably likely to join Brown, John T. Clay, and Eli Jordan, making a good living as a nationally significant horse trainer and trader, mentoring young Black horsemen.

But racing itself seemed to be changing, its customs crystalizing into code under pressure from the most powerful owners of the East. In 1893, James R. Keene took the lead in pressing for a national governing body for racing that would be controlled by horse owners, rather than track operators, who had previously led the effort for such national leadership. He called for fellow owners to meet at the Hoffman House in Manhattan to organize such a group. Keene spoke to those assembled about the danger that racing might end up under state regulation. The answer, familiar to the men in the room from their businesses, was to self-regulate, to leverage the economic and social power of Thoroughbred owners to keep their sport firmly under their control. Thus the modern Jockey Club was born and ultimately given the power to license horsemen, appoint officials, and interpret and enforce the rules of racing. "It should be autocratic," summed up Walter Vosburgh, who served as the body's secretary, possessing absolute authority over all the tracks that it deemed worthy to race under its auspices.[79] The club took office space on Fifth Avenue and went to work.[80] When states did regulate racing, the club used the personal prestige and authority of its members to ensure that, to a large degree, official regulatory commissions worked in tandem with it. As the club consolidated its power, a few men would come to control breeding, racing, licensing, and regulation—akin to the strategies of vertical integration they used in their offices to build industry-dominating conglomerates.[81]

Trainers and jockeys worked in a world fundamentally based on patronage, which meant they always served at the pleasure of the powerful. That had not changed. The new system formalized that reality and its vulnerabilities, however, since the Jockey Club and its Western partner the Turf Congress had absolute discretion to issue or refuse licenses to ride or train at the tracks they governed, and the process now officially required the applicant

to "have a good reputation . . . and to be . . . fitted for the avoca-
tion."[82] Those were subjective qualifications that allowed the governing bodies to police who worked in racing.

Murphy and his fellow African American jockeys do not seem
to have had difficulty getting licensed in the 1890s. He regularly
renewed his qualification.[83] But the power of the Jockey Club
brought into sharp relief the patterns of authority that had governed racing since the antebellum period and how precarious they
could make Black men's position. When James R. Keene chaired
an investigative committee for the club, his son remembered, he
took testimony from a groom who made him laugh by abasing
himself as "a flat-footed, no-account loafer, an' a crap-shootin'
son of a bitch." As the committee members roared with laughter,
Keene poked his assistant to request, "Buy me that nigger. . . . I
like him."[84] Racing had given Murphy and his colleagues a platform
to model the possibilities of equality, because the sport was built
on a history of Black labor and expertise. But that very history
also carried enduring legacies of slavery and racial subordination.

Though the authority of racing patriarchs rose to new heights,
the prestige of African American jockeys seemed poised to continue. "There are myriads of diminutive colored boys in the South
who want to become jockeys, after the style of Isaac Murphy,"
reported the *Louisville Courier Journal.*[85] Willie Simms, originally
from Augusta, Georgia, rose to the top of New York racing in the
early 1890s, riding for W. L. Scott, president of the Erie Railroad.[86]
In the winter of 1895, he visited the Murphys in Lexington before
he headed to England to ride for Mike Dwyer.[87] There he would
impress British horsemen, as he perched with short stirrups over
his mount's withers. Simms's trip to England would go down
in history as a major milestone in the evolution of the modern
jockey's seat.[88]

Closer to home, a new generation of Black horsemen like Monk

Overton, Lonnie Clayton, Tom Britton, and James "Soup" Perkins rode at the top level.[89] Perkins's father worked at the Lexington trotting track, and James was galloping Thoroughbreds in the morning when he was ten years old.[90] He nearly swept the card at Lexington one afternoon in 1893 and supported his family with his earnings at the age of thirteen. Mrs. Perkins used the money to buy a house and an investment property, setting her family up for a secure future in a way America Murphy Burns would have understood.[91] Later that year, Perkins would sign a contract to ride for four thousand dollars annually.[92] In 1895, a nationally praised professional, he took the Kentucky Derby with Halma.[93]

But even if Black men continued at the highest level, their success seemed an increasingly uneasy matter. "The race question almost forces itself on one's attention," conceded the *Spirit of the Times*. "There is no use in mincing matters, but here in the West the main reliance for thoroughly skilled and capable riding material is on the colored article."[94] The same author, touting the accomplishments of Pike Barnes, Monk Overton, Tom Britton, and Robert "Tiny" Williams, was "sorry to state that a quartette of noted and skillful white jockeys is lacking."[95] In 1891, a small group of white riders at Latonia began complaining that they were being discriminated against in favor of Black competitors and threatened to gang up on African American jockeys. Nothing came of it—in fact, at least one white jockey was ruled off the course for his efforts—but this kind of open complaint was new.[96]

Jockeys in general came in for grumbles about the status they accrued. But while fans and journalists sometimes demonstrated reflexive discomfort with jockeys when they acted like professionals, rather than like retainers of wealthy patrons, that unease edged into malice when it came to young Black men. The *Thoroughbred Record* complained that Fred Taral behaved like a peer of James R. Keene. But even worse, "Soup" Perkins "undoubtedly considers himself to be just a little bit better than his employers, who have thrown into his way the means of making a lucrative living. . . . And Lonny Clayton. . . . That boy has no compunction in assuming the dignity of a forty-five-year-old horse owner and reveling in the thought that the men have to recognize his merit."[97] When young Black men acted as if they were entitled to respect, they weren't just asserting a claim to equality. Instead, white journalists insisted, they were enjoying a situation in which they could somehow compel white people to treat them as superiors. In looking at those young men, reporters revealed that they were incapable of seeing a society based on equality. And since hierarchy was inevitable, it was imperative to be on top.

Racing men, like those around them, could feel the consequences of decades of Black activism. By the 1890s, Black people could look back on decades of determined efforts to replace racial subordination with multiracial democracy. In the 1870s, William Walker gritted his teeth and rode under the threat of lynching; he figured he had no choice. But in the 1890s, when a starter at Latonia called Jerry Chorn "you d—d black nigger," Chorn cursed back at him, because, as he said, "That made me mad, and it wasn't the first time either."[98] Chorn got suspended, but his response revealed what had happened over the years Isaac Murphy had been riding. Black men sometimes angrily demanded they be treated with respect, precisely because it seemed possible they might be able to secure the rights they were denied.

White Americans responded to that possibility with a reign of extralegal terror. At the spring meeting in Nashville in 1892, most of the crowd at the races deserted the action to join a lynch mob that took a Black man named Ephraim Grizzard from jail, hanged him off the Woodland Street Bridge, and riddled his body with bullets.[99] (The Tennessee Titans' stadium looms over the bridge today.) Monk Overton and other African American jockeys were riding at Nashville that day and must have had their vulnerability forcibly brought home to them. A few years later, the *New York Tribune* insisted that lynching was "always infamous, always inexcusable." But if Lonnie Clayton had ridden in the South the way he had in the Brooklyn Handicap, he would have been lynched, as "hundreds of colored men have been lynched . . . for offenses less irritating and exasperating."[100] They weren't *condoning* racial violence, but they thought it might be *justified* in this case. As the violence surged, white Americans found ways to excuse it, to make it seem normal or inevitable.

As usual, efforts to suppress Black citizenship went hand in hand with insistence that it wasn't what most Black people wanted anyway. As civil rights activism continued, so did efforts to wrap men like Isaac Murphy in the narratives of the minstrel show and the sentimental plantation saga. In 1894, he got an offer to go on the road with *The Derby Winner,* a play by a St. Louis sportswriter. The play featured the exploits of the owner of a racehorse named Missouri Girl and his attempts to protect her from hostile gamblers. Meanwhile, his fiancée suspected him of being unfaithful to her, because she kept hearing about his connection to another woman. It took most of the play for her to realize that Missouri Girl was a horse. That kind of plotting may explain why the *Nebraska State Journal*'s drama critic, a young Willa Cather, opined that the play just gave the viewer "that tired feeling."[101] But the show toured the Midwest and Northeast throughout 1894 and 1895, and other reviewers oohed and aahed over the big production numbers, featuring Black characters singing and dancing, and the live racing scene featuring retired stars of the turf.[102] Freeland was the show's greatest equine attraction, and "as Murphy used to ride the great son of Longfellow years ago, he was selected as a drawing card to pilot Freeland once more in the fierce contests on the stage."[103] Thus were the victories of less than a decade earlier pushed back into an indeterminate past, safely over and now fictionalized. Murphy never actually joined the company, though he was slated to appear in a performance and promotional event when the play came to Lexington.[104] Going into show business would be a way of signaling gracious retirement, and he had no intention of retiring.

But continuing was a struggle. In June 1894, Murphy rode Myrtle at Latonia and repeated, in less spectacular fashion, his performance on Firenze a few years earlier. The judges suspended him for a month.[105] Murphy was bitterly aware that fans now reflexively assumed he rode drunk and that their assumptions were rooted in racism. As he told a reporter, "When I won it was all right, but when I lost, and when not on the best horse, they would say, 'there, that nigger is drunk again.'"[106] All his losses, his flaws, even his bad luck would be chalked up to his Blackness. He would be turned into an object lesson: no Black man could ever be more than race dictated, no matter how extraordinarily talented he was.

In January 1893, Murphy made his will, "realizing the hazardous nature of my business." He left everything to Lucy.[107] In 1895, he announced that he would work freelance and that he could ride at 106 pounds. It seems likely that he desperately wanted to get back in the saddle and even more likely that he was fooling himself about whether dropping so much weight would be physically possible.[108] He started that March in Nashville, going back to the circuit through the South and Midwest that had first nurtured his career. But after a few weeks, he still hadn't had a mount.[109] He did pick up the ride on Lazzarone in the Brooklyn Handicap and seemed as polished as ever, finishing behind his old friend Tony Hamilton on Hornpipe.[110] When Lazzarone returned to win the Suburban commandingly, defeating the brilliant Domino, his victory seemed partially due to first-time blinkers, donned at Murphy's suggestion.[111] But Hamilton had replaced Murphy in the saddle, much to Murphy's chagrin. Hamilton himself said he would have refused to ride, if he had known Murphy had thought he was booked. Later that summer Murphy rode Rey El Santa Anita, E. J. Baldwin's American Derby winner, in New York for his old employer, only to have the horse turn in a terrible performance. Baldwin immediately asked his jockey what had happened, and Murphy said he believed the horse had been doped. Trainer Sam Hildreth hotly denied it, insisting that Murphy had been drunk. Hildreth would go on to train the winners of seven Triple Crown races and to lead American trainers in annual winnings nine times. But Baldwin, used to taking Murphy's word, sided with his jockey.[112]

Murphy was still a consummate horseman, whose opinion was sought and deferred to. But that didn't protect him from losing mounts or from being regularly accused of alcohol abuse. He must have been tired and discouraged. In 1895, he had twenty mounts. He won twice and hit the board an additional eight times. But he couldn't make a career out of that.[113] At the fall meeting in Lexington that November, he coaxed home Tupto, a notoriously sulky horse, for both the final win and the final ride of his career.[114]

Why did he not quit? Maybe he worried that his training operation wouldn't take off and figured he had to maximize his earning potential for as long as he could. Maybe he just didn't feel like himself when he wasn't riding. He wouldn't be the first or last athlete who couldn't quite bear to stop, even when his body betrayed him. But there was also the most basic reason. He needed the money.

In the fall of 1895, Lexington merchants sued Murphy for failure to pay them for everyday items like flour and horse feed and clothing.[115] He and Lucy had recently sold their first house on Megowan Street, which they had rented out for years, and mortgaged the property they had purchased near Gratz Park. In December 1895 they sold that to get out from under the debt.[116] The purchaser of the Megowan Street house was Gus Luigart, who operated the English Kitchen, a restaurant and entertainment venue that featured "200 fans in perpetual motion and 5,000 gallons of water flowing over a petrified Nymph."[117] His father Fred had been a Lexington grain dealer, while his brother George established himself in the grocery and saloon business.[118] Not only did Gus buy the Megowan Street house, but on February 9, 1896, he loaned the Murphys fifty-five hundred dollars in exchange for a mortgage on the house they lived in.[119]

Murphy was sick that day, just as he had been for several weeks, and the grinding worries about money must have made the situation worse. On the night of February 11, Lucy sent for the doctor. Just after midnight, he died.[120] His death certificate listed heart failure as the cause. He was barely thirty-five years old.[121]

On Sunday, February 16, hundreds of mourners gathered at the home on Third Street. They filled the house and stood in the yard to pay tribute. White horsemen were in the crowd as Reverend S. P. Young of the First Baptist Church performed the funeral. Ed Corrigan and Fred Taral sent flowers. But when it came time to bear the body to its final resting place in the African American cemetery on Seventh Street, Murphy's Black friends and colleagues were the ones who went with him. His pallbearers included John T. Clay, Edward Brown, and William Walker, along with other Black horsemen who had been his friends like Charles Anderson and Lee Christy. He was buried with the rites of the Black Masons of Lexington's Lincoln Lodge, who honored him in death as "one of our most faithful and worthy brothers."[122]

That spring, the Supreme Court would hand down its decision in *Plessy v. Ferguson*, ruling that segregated train travel was constitutional, so long as accommodations of equal quality were provided for all passengers. De jure segregation would now bear the highest court's official stamp of approval. Alone, Kentucky's John Marshall Harlan dissented. Segregation, he argued, was one of the "badges of slavery" that the Thirteenth Amendment had sought to stamp out. The Fourteenth Amendment, "which added greatly to the dignity and glory of American citizenship," with its insistence on due process and equal protection, rendered segregation doubly anathema. "Our Constitution is color-blind, and neither knows nor tolerates classes among citizens," Harlan magnificently asserted, as he predicted that the *Plessy* decision would bring in tidal waves of violence against Black people. Americans boasted of their great freedom. "But it is difficult to reconcile that boast with a state of the law which, practically, puts the brand of servitude and degradation upon a large class of our fellow citizens, our equals before the law. The thin disguise of 'equal' accommodations for passengers in railroad coaches will not mislead anyone, nor atone for the wrong this day done."[123]

CHAPTER 5

———

Afterlives

L UCY MURPHY REMAINED with her mother in the house on Third Street. She still occasionally hosted friends; she threw a garden party the next year in honor of distinguished guests at the Colored Fair.[1] There was some speculation in the papers that perhaps Murphy's so-often reported fortune hadn't survived his death, but the gossip mostly didn't make it into print.[2]

Out of print, the truth was ugly. With Murphy's death, Lucy's income had largely disappeared, and, in the years afterward, her finances tangled into disaster. George Luigart sued her, claiming that he had loaned her fifty-five hundred dollars in February 1898 and that she had not paid him back. As a result, he insisted, he was now entitled to lay claim to the Third Street property, which she had used as collateral. By Lucy's account, Gus Luigart had loaned her and her husband money in 1895. The extremely high interest he charged made it impossible to pay back what they owed, so they renegotiated a new loan a few days before Murphy died. When that loan came due in February 1898, Lucy extended it. She asserted that the Luigarts had threatened that they would foreclose on the mortgage and throw her out of her home if she didn't consent to the extension and the transfer of the debt to George Luigart. Now the Luigarts needed cash, so they were suing, when they were at fault as predatory lenders. The Luigarts denied collusion and usury and insisted that Lucy Murphy and her husband had dealt with them freely. George Luigart claimed to have loaned Lucy the money to clear her debt to his brother in exchange for the mortgage. Meanwhile, the city of Lexington demanded payment of back taxes on the property.[3]

In 1898 the Luigarts had purchased a canning factory in Lexington, hoping to mass-produce soup. But their investment required work on the factory equipment, like the giant copper kettles that had to be shipped from Cincinnati, and they faced delays in getting the business off the ground. Their problems square with Lucy's claim about their urgent need for cash.[4] Lucy presented herself as a widow who had dutifully signed where her husband had told her, with no knowledge of what she was agreeing to. She may have been hiding behind convenient pleas of feminine helplessness, or she may have been truly ignorant, a wife who had always deferred to her husband. It didn't matter. In 1900, the court ordered the Third Street property "sold at the front door of the court house." George Luigart was the buyer, for a bargain price. He turned the property over to his brother.[5]

Where had the money gone? The best answer may be one that Lonnie Clayton offered for himself two years after Murphy's death. Riding was seasonal and dangerous work, and he supported family and a small group of assistants and friends year-round. His job required frequent and expensive travel. He never intended to be extravagant, but the money just went.[6] And Murphy had been seeking to secure his future in the famously risky business of talent-spotting young horses, a venture that always involves significant outlay and inevitable sunk cost. When vaunted talent-spotter Edward Brown died in 1906, he was also widely reported to have somehow lost his money, despite his famous roll of cash.[7] Murphy and his friends, like so many athletes after them, were trying to build what we would call generational wealth in the course of one generation. J. B. Haggin and James R. Keene didn't carry rolls of cash, except on a whim, because they had their funds securely salted away, accruing interest and dividends. Even when men born enslaved managed to make so much money, it was still finite, especially as they tried to provide for futures, families, friends without many other sources of income to fall back on. And so Lucy Murphy lost her home exactly as America Murphy Burns had.[8]

Lucy died of pneumonia in 1910.[9] The pallbearers who laid her to rest beside her husband included old friends from the track, like Charles Anderson, John T. Clay, and Robert F. "Senator" Bell.[10] The Bell family took in Lucy's mother, Susan Osborn, who was living with them when she died in 1919. Clay, who had taken care of Lucy's estate, notified the authorities of her mother's death.[11]

Edward Brown's son Lee L. Brown went on to be a teacher, journalist, and civil rights activist, who always honored the memory of his father's skill and what it had provided for his family.[12] John T. Clay was for years the official race starter at the Colored Fair Association.[13] He remained staunch in his loyalty to African American fraternal organizations and to the Republican Party, attending conventions and canvassing for years.[14] His sons, John and Barack, participated in Lexington's celebration of the anniversary of emancipation, playing "an instrumental duet." Along with them as a piano soloist was Abe Perry, the son and namesake of Murphy's old friend.[15] When he grew up, the younger Perry became a doctor, and his daughter, Julia Amanda Perry, would go on to win Guggenheim Fellowships as an internationally acclaimed composer. On his draft card, the doctor carefully penned his full name, Abraham Murphy Perry.[16] Even after his death, Mur-

A running of the Ashland Oaks at the Lexington track, where Isaac Murphy and his neighbors started their careers. Keeneland Library McClure Collection.

phy survived in the dreams and achievements of his friends and neighbors.

Antigambling forces in New York, led by Governor Charles Evans Hughes, finally succeeded in shutting down racing there in 1911, in what the great racetrack character J. S. A. McDonald called "a deathblow at gracious living in America."[17] California and Illinois tracks closed around the same time. The Lexington track stumbled through the 1890s in perpetually cash-strapped condition, shuttering temporarily in 1898. In 1908, the Louisville city government banned bookmaking at Churchill Downs, and the management had to resort to what McDonald gloomily called "the sordid pari-mutuel."[18] The machines saved the track, and the crowds sang "Auld Lang Syne" along with a forty-piece orchestra at Belmont Park when New York racing returned in 1913. Though the Lexington track closed for good in 1933, its legacy continued at Keeneland, on the western end of town, where some of its signature races are still run.[19]

Racing changed, but it continued, and Black men continued with it. Lexington native Jimmy Winkfield won the Kentucky Derby in 1901 and 1902 and finished second in a squeaker in 1903, barely missing Isaac Murphy's record. He quickly followed Anthony Hamilton and other jockeys to Europe, where he rode with splendid success in Poland and Russia and finished his career a highly decorated trainer in France.[20]

Behind Winkfield came Jimmy Lee. Raised on the track at New Orleans, the kid had one ambition. "His sole goal is to be a greater jockey than was Isaac Murphy, and it begins to look as if he is sure to realize that hope," reported the *Louisville Times* in 1907.[21] That year Lee racked up 217 wins out of more than a thousand mounts.[22] At the Louisville spring meeting, he was in the money almost 43 percent of the time.[23] That June he rode the winners of all six races on one afternoon card at Churchill Downs.[24] When he won the Latonia Derby that summer with The Abbot, the fans screamed and rushed him, in "the involuntary expression of a crowd of people, who love the turf . . . and who had suddenly become convinced that here was the best rider in the land."[25]

At the New Orleans spring meeting of 1908, white jockeys ganged up on Lee. They prevented him from getting to the front in races, tried to run him into the fence or bring his horse down.

They were hoping either to drive him from the track or stop employers from risking their horses in his care. Lee confronted one of the offenders on a downtown street and told him he wouldn't stand for it. But he was facing something bigger than a few jealous rivals. Joe Notter, one of the top jockeys of the East, would win the Belmont that year with James R. Keene's Colin and ride Regret to win the first Kentucky Derby for a filly in 1915. In 1907, Lee had easily topped him in the standings. Notter acknowledged that Lee was probably the best jockey he had ever competed against, but "he and the other white boys did not like to have the negro riding in the same races with them."[26] Lee was a casualty of a recurrent campaign in the first decade of the twentieth century, in which white riders tried to eliminate Black competition. And like Notter, they bluntly acknowledged that their feelings were rooted in racism and, presumably, their desire to get the mounts and the purse money that belonged to their Black opponents. Jimmy Winkfield had gone to Europe in part because of a "jockey war" in Chicago that had badly injured his mount and landed him in the hospital with a dislocated hip. Now Jimmy Lee's career ended at its apex, as trainers and owners grew reluctant to entrust their precious charges to a man with a target on his back.[27]

Fairly rapidly, Black riders' numbers dwindled.[28] Newspapers began pointing out that there were fewer Black trainers as well, outside of a few older men like Dudley Allen.[29] Fewer Black riders meant fewer men like Murphy and Edward Brown, who had transitioned to training and could mentor young jockeys. The pipeline that had funneled young Black men from groom to jockey to trainer, a pipeline that had existed for centuries, in slavery and in freedom, slowed to a trickle. It may have been convenient to point to white riders as the villains, but jockeys are ultimately dependent on the people who employ them. Owners and trainers control who gets the best mounts, so white jockeys must have had at least implicit sanction for their actions from their employers, as the *New York Times* hinted in 1900.[30] For decades racing had supposedly shamed other sports in its refusal to draw the color line, and white jockeys had not openly complained. What was the explanation for "a great amount of prejudice existing now that was not apparent a few years ago"?[31]

White commentators like the sportswriter Hugh Keough were sometimes gratingly honest about the answer. Black riders, he explained, usually carefully calibrated how they acted around white people. Those men he had no quarrel with. But Black fans came to the track to celebrate jockeys' achievements and sat in the grandstand and talked as loudly as anybody else. They literally took up space in a place he thought of as his. And in doing so, they were "flaunting . . . the fifteenth amendment." They were forcing him to acknowledge them as people who were entitled to go on a public outing, to cheer noisily, and to vote. They were citizens, not tolerated subordinates. When Black jockeys won, he complained, the praise they received "was accepted as a compliment to the entire race and the porter that made up your berth took his share of it and assumed a perkiness that got on your nerves."[32] It seems unlikely that railroad porters, dependent on the goodwill of white patrons, publicly demonstrated any emotion they thought might imperil their livelihood. Their professional survival depended on the kind of meticulous self-regulation that Keough assumed was his due. He imagined their glee because he knew it must be there. He explicitly acknowledged what Black and white commentators had believed for decades about Black jockeys: they represented Black people's demands for full citizenship in America. He viscerally rejected equality for Black people, so Black jockeys were dangerous, and their disappearance was for the best.

The end could be horribly painful. Albert Isom, who, like Isaac Murphy, had ridden for Jack Chinn, walked into a Lexington pawnshop and bought a gun and cartridges. He loaded the pistol and shot himself in the head in front of the clerk.[33] The prominent jockey Tom Britton, one of Murphy's circle of friends and the brother of civil rights activist Mary Britton, had been working with horses since he was eight years old. At twenty-nine, he could no longer find a job on the racetrack. He rented a room in Cincinnati and drank carbolic acid. He left a note for his wife to tell her he loved her and would never see her again, because he knew he was going to hell.[34] In 1911, James Perkins died of heart failure at thirty-three after years of trying to scrape a living on the track. The obituary writer at the Lexington paper noted, "He was awkward everywhere save on the horse."[35] There he had been graceful, a Kentucky Derby winner with a brilliant future. Out of the saddle, he was one of millions of Black men, struggling to survive as hope flickered. Each tragedy was weighted with its own particular balance of grief and anger and misery. But so much despair in such a small professional and personal world is a stark reminder of the devastation of Jim Crow.

Hugh Keough, in the same article in which he seethed about the relationship between Black fans and Black athletes, insisted that racism had nothing to do with the decline in the number of Black riders. The number of Black jockeys had dropped dramatically, he acknowledged, but that "cannot be laid at the door of race prejudice." It was simply impossible for Black and white men to "mix in such close quarters," so segregation had to be the rule in stables. He ignored the generations of Black and white men working together that even casual racing fans would know about. You could always get a few Black kids to help out around the barn. It was easy, racing magazines pronounced, since a potential employer would only have to deal with a single mother, deserted by a deadbeat partner, not two concerned white parents who might worry about the safety of stable work. But "a little success turns their heads and makes them useless" after a while.[36] Reliable workers were white, and the "survival of the fittest" must hold sway.[37] Biological racism and bigoted assumptions about Black families combined in a toxic brew that supposedly made segregation inevitable.

Frequently, journalists professed confusion about why Black riders had so suddenly disappeared from high-class racing. "Almost as great a mystery as the total disappearance of the passenger pigeon," they called it.[38] "Can anyone explain?" they asked in elaborate bafflement.[39] The color line, after all, wasn't real; the glory of athletics was that all competitors were equal.[40] That was Jimmy Lee's problem, sighed the *Daily Racing Form*. "There is no doubt that when easy in his mind Lee is a skillful jockey but he too frequently gets an idea into his head that the white riders are conspiring to injure him."[41]

Black riders had to be gotten rid of because their success had real consequences, and that was dangerous. But actually they weren't gotten rid of; they disappeared because their race inevitably rendered them unable to do the jobs they had always done. And no one knew why they disappeared. It was a mystery. They might claim it had something to do with race, but that was just an excuse. All those overlapping explanations and denials were obviously illogical but powerful precisely because they transcended logic and instead provided something fans and readers wanted at the turn of the twentieth century. In *The Fire Next Time,* James Baldwin considers this kind of rapid-fire justification and concealment, fueled by the desire to maintain structures that hurt people but not to feel guilty about it. "I know . . . and this is the crime of which I accuse my country and my countrymen, and for which neither I nor time nor history will ever forgive them, that they have destroyed and are destroying hundreds of thousands of lives and do not know it and do not want to know it. . . . But it is not permissible that the authors of devastation should also be innocent. It is the innocence which constitutes the crime."[42] When white Americans asked whatever had happened to Black riders, they protested their innocence and compounded the crime.

In Murphy's hometown, white citizens vehemently insisted on that kind of innocence. The ladies of the United Daughters of the Confederacy complained when Lexington theaters staged ever-popular adaptations of *Uncle Tom's Cabin*. They worried that depictions of slavery might make white children uncomfortable and cause community division. So strenuous were their protests that they managed to get the state of Kentucky to pass a law in 1906 that illegalized the showing of any production "that excites race prejudice." In 1910, the law would prevent the screening of footage of African American fighter Jack Johnson defeating Jim Jeffries for the heavyweight championship of the world. But it certainly did not stop screenings of *Birth of a Nation*, the D. W. Griffith blockbuster that celebrated the Reconstruction-era Ku Klux Klan and inspired the founding of the modern version of the organization. The film shattered records in Lexington, seating almost fifteen hundred audience members a day. It returned to town repeatedly in the 1910s and 1920s, playing to packed houses at the Ben Ali, a downtown theater in which J. B. Haggin was the principal investor.[43]

In a world of stories like *Birth of a Nation*, what stories survived about Isaac Murphy into the twentieth century? Decades after he died, white racing men still spoke of him with reverence. One journalist remembered in 1920, "As he vaulted into the saddle of a great race horse on a great occasion . . . he looked as handsome as Phaeton must have looked when he stepped into his chariot to guide the sun."[44] Even after World War II, older fans remembered "what a thrill a boy got out of actually seeing Isaac

Murphy close up, and maybe hearing him say something."[45] But reverence always coexisted with assumptions about how Black people could be depicted and understood. When the *Louisville Courier Journal* celebrated the history of the Derby in 1928, including Murphy's record-setting three wins, he appeared in a drawing on the front page as an anonymous caricature, with inked-in flat features and huge, white pop-eyes.[46] Murphy was supposedly the inspiration for the character of Asbestos in Ken Kling's racetrack-set comic strip *Joe and Asbestos*. But until the Congress of Racial Equality asked Kling to reconsider his depiction of the character in the 1960s, Asbestos had "an 'eightball' head with white, round, bulging eyes; thick, white, clown-shaped lips . . . totally black skin."[47]

In Black communities, Murphy continued his work as a marker of uplift and possibility, even in death. The *Indianapolis Freeman*, in its coverage of Jack Johnson, compared the two men.[48] When Johnson won the heavyweight championship and unleashed a torrent of joy in Black America, he remembered Isaac Murphy had been his boyhood hero.[49] *Abbott's Monthly*, a magazine that shared an owner with the *Chicago Defender*, interviewed John T. Clay and Charles Anderson about Murphy in the same issue in which they profiled Universal Negro Improvement Association leader and international Black activist Marcus Garvey.[50] James Weldon Johnson lauded Murphy as the "most highly finished American horseman who ever rode a race." He was probably repeating local gossip, but, if so, then Murphy's legend still lived on in African American communities in New York in the 1930s.[51] In 1940, Murphy starred in a diorama at the American Negro Exposition in Chicago, held to celebrate the seventy-fifth anniversary of emancipation.[52] "He didn't go in no back doors," summed up Jo Jones, Count Basie's iconic drummer.[53] Of course, Murphy must have done so at some point in his life, but he hadn't always, and he had helped people dream of a world where no one did. That was what mattered.

In the racing season, the caretaker of Lexington's African American cemetery told *Abbott's Monthly*, so many people came to visit Murphy's grave that he had put up a small sign.[54] But most white residents had essentially forgotten it. In the 1950s, newspapers casually circulated a report that Murphy had been buried in the family plot of William Cottrill of Mobile, the owner of Buchanan, Murphy's first Kentucky Derby winner. The account was a classic example of the kind of story into which Murphy had been slotted throughout his life: the faithful Black man whose achievements with horses made him part of an intimate circle for powerful white men, the latter-day manifestation of the faithful slave. The story was particularly ironic given the brief and contentious business relationship Murphy had with Cottrill. The report drew the attention of a few people in Lexington, including Amelia Buckley, librarian of the major repository of racing history housed at Keeneland, and journalist Frank Borries. And as Borries observed, the account of Murphy's burial "was received with amusement in Lexington colored circles," where people who had known Murphy still lived.[55]

Borries and Buckley went to work finding Murphy's grave. The records of the cemetery had been destroyed in a fire, so Borries turned to local African Americans, asking them what they and their families remembered.[56] He spent years on the phone and in people's living rooms, essentially doing research as an outsider in his own town. Finally, Eugene Webster, who lived in the housing project the city had constructed on the site of the old Lexington track, contacted Borries and offered to lead him to the grave. In 1909, Webster had been galloping horses at the Lexington track, where his father had worked before him and known Murphy, when a group of horsemen passed the hat to put up a marker. It was a small concrete pillar, built around an anchoring pipe. It was blank, because they didn't know how to engrave the surface. But they knew what it meant. They just didn't want his grave to be lost, Webster explained. "We wanted to do something for him."[57]

So what was to be done about Murphy, now that Borries had rediscovered the grave for white people? What happened to Murphy's grave was inextricably bound up with responses to the civil rights movement, with attempts to celebrate Black history as a method of channeling present demands for equality. Borries's account of his search ultimately ended up on the desk of Ted Worner, the indefatigable promotion manager for Kentucky Club tobacco. Worner decided that his client would sponsor a ceremonial reburial for Murphy. He suggested that an ideal new site for the jockey's grave would be a Lexington park where Man o' War's bones already rested.[58]

The disinterment itself was not ceremonial. Borries and a few others, along with local cemetery worker Benny Railey, dug in the vicinity of the concrete marker and hoped for the best. They found no casket and no recognizable remains. Local gossip had it that Murphy had been buried in a very expensive coffin, which had been stolen by grave robbers. In the end, the expedition collected only a small box of dirt and a metal handle.[59]

On May 4, 1967, the Thursday before that year's Kentucky Derby, the mayor of Lexington and other local officials, along with representatives of the Jockey Club and Churchill Downs, celebrated the reburial with a small crowd.[60] Andrew Hatcher, who had been the first African American to work in the White House press office, told the audience, "In these times of civil rights controversy, it is highly fitting that a southern state honor a Negro who was a great man."[61]

"Civil rights controversy" loomed large around the ceremony.

Alongside the Lexington paper's report of the memorial was a notice that Muhammad Ali's lawyers had filed an appeal in his case to be considered a conscientious objector to the Vietnam War. The paper conspicuously called him Cassius Clay, the birth name Ali had rejected after his public embrace of the Nation of Islam.[62] Ali's antiwar stance would set off a chain reaction, as other athletes he inspired, including 1968 Olympians Tommie Smith and John Carlos, would use their victories to call attention to the consequences of racism in the United States and abroad. Ted Worner told the press that he liked to think about Murphy as the antidote to Ali, a sports hero with a story that was "warm and nice."[63] Murphy was a Black athlete who could be safely celebrated, an implicit rebuke to his activist successors.

But as the 1967 Kentucky Derby approached, there were controversies closer to home as well. That spring, Louisville was locked in a battle over housing. Civil rights leaders, including Martin Luther King, Jr., his brother A. D. King, and Ali himself led Black marchers through residential neighborhoods where African Americans could not buy homes. They faced white mobs who carried Confederate flags and threw rocks. A few wore the robes of the Ku Klux Klan. The Louisville city government blamed the protests on "outside agitators" and refused to pass an open housing ordinance. Louisville police deputized white counter-protestors to load Black demonstrators into paddy wagons, and the city trumped up excuses to put movement leaders in jail. City officials were desperate to conceal the upheaval or somehow suspend it in time for the Derby.[64]

Activists split over whether they should seek to stop the race. Some saw the threat of a shutdown as the best bargaining tactic they had. Dick Gregory, who had led marching schoolchildren in Birmingham against police dogs, shrugged, "I ain't going to lay down in front of a horse myself, but there's a lot of cats that will.

If it comes to closing the Derby up, we'll just have to close it up."[65] Five young men ran out in front of the horses in one of the races at Churchill Downs on the Tuesday before the Derby.[66] But other leaders argued that letting the race run unimpeded would serve as a gesture of good faith and help in negotiations with city leaders. The *Louisville Defender*, the mouthpiece of older Black leadership in the city, agreed that the Derby was not the place to demonstrate. Publishing photographs of Isaac Murphy alongside reports of his reburial, it reminded its readers that the Derby was a part of Black history.[67] In the end, organizers, including Martin Luther King, brokered an agreement not to protest the race.[68] But the governor still called out the National Guard, who were at the track to see Proud Clarion go off at 30 to 1 and win by a length.[69] The goodwill that activists hoped to foster didn't turn out to be worth much, and the marches continued. But so did assiduous voter registration drives. In the fall of 1967, Black voters helped to unseat eleven of twelve aldermen, and that December the city passed an open housing ordinance. In 1968, the state of Kentucky followed suit, and later that year Congress would follow up with national legislation.[70]

The Lexington paper, as it celebrated Murphy's reburial, complained bitterly about the fair housing demonstrators. They were a "mob," and the only proper response was to turn the "full power of the government" on them.[71] Letters to the editor applauded this stance and excoriated the demonstrators, who were asserting that the law should mandate equal treatment in the market and in public facilities.[72] It was a debate that Murphy would have recognized, because it was the same debate he and his mother had lived through. What did the Fourteenth Amendment actually mean? Did it mean that Black people could live, travel, eat, learn, and sleep freely and equally with white people? Or did it not? Were they full citizens? Or were they not?

White journalists preferred to assume they knew what Murphy would have thought of such debates. Indeed, they explicitly said Murphy would never have been involved in activism. He had faced adversity but never openly expressed anger about it, and he had been successful, which proved that protest would never be the right response to injustice. He should inspire everyone as "a giant object lesson in the American Way."[73] One suggested that it was best, after all, that there had been no body to put in the new grave. Murphy's very bones would have been dishonored by exposure to civil rights protest.[74] The new memorial marker was lettered with a quote from the obituary L. P. Tarlton had written for Murphy. Tarlton was himself quoting Alexander Pope: "Honour and shame from no condition rise. Act well your part, there all the honour lies." The epitaph smacked unmistakably of the same theme that the memorial coverage was shot through with: relief at a Black celebrity who had supposedly distinguished himself by accepting that he had to live his life within certain limits.

When the state built the Kentucky Horse Park in the 1970s, Murphy and Man o' War's monuments were moved there. This time a few people suggested that Murphy and Lucy could be honored together, perhaps in Lexington Cemetery, with appropriate memorial and historical markers. It at least made more sense than moving Murphy's memorial considerably north of Lexington, along with a horse he had no connection to. But after minimal debate, officials went along with the Horse Park plan. It would be too difficult, they said, to find Lucy's grave and too expensive to move her remains.[75] Murphy had "moved to a better neighborhood," celebrated one journalist.[76]

Man o' War was reburied under a huge statue, with some of his greatest progeny, including Triple Crown winner War Admiral, buried around him. Murphy's marker stood nearby. The jockey "completes the family," an Associated Press story explained.[77]

Officials had asked Mary Harbut, the widow of Will Harbut, Man o' War's final and beloved groom and the defining curator of the horse's legend, if she would consent to have his body reinterred there. She understood that it was intended to be an honor, but, as her granddaughter explained, she said, "'People stay with people and animals with animals,' and that was that."[78] Mrs. Harbut quietly asserted that her husband's family and friends were more important than his job. But there was no one left alive to say the same for Isaac Murphy, to point out that what was offered as an honor erased the bonds he shared with other people.

Murphy remained celebrated in a cursory way, noted in reference books with his winning percentages and his birth and death dates, the same words of praise from his contemporaries recycled. As he became larger than life, he cast a shadow that obscured the Black men he had worked with. As late as the 1990s, African American trainer Dale Mills expressed surprise that other Black jockeys had won major American races. "Basically, what I know is what I read about Isaac Murphy." "For a long time, that is all anyone knew," followed up the *Baltimore Sun*.[79] Or it was all some people remembered.

But Black people never left the racetrack. As William Doyle would tell an oral history interviewer, in the Louisville neighborhood he grew up in, blocks from Churchill Downs, everyone ended up somehow associated with the racing industry. "It was a conversation piece everyday," he explained. "Talking about a horse."[80] Like generations before them, Larry Bonafon agreed, they had lapped up the tutelage of older Black horsemen. "The desire to be around them was overwhelming because the things they taught you, and becoming a skilled horseman was a desire for the young men in those days. I think that we looked forward to being considered knowing the game, knowing the horse."[81] But even for those who reached that goal, racing still kept up significant barriers to the kind of career Murphy had enjoyed.

The great African American exercise rider Marshall Lilly galloped some of the mightiest champions of the twentieth century, including Colin and Regret, the two most famous mounts of jockey Joe Notter, the spokesman for white riders who ganged up against Jimmy Lee.[82] Notter entered American racing's Hall of Fame in 1963. Lilly never got famous beyond the backstretch. Dick Spiller, who trained around the country just as his father had trained at the old Lexington track before it closed, remembered traveling with his string. You could ride with other passengers or with the horses on the train, he recalled, and he preferred to ride with the animals, to avoid segregated seating. When he drove a horse van, he kept a wary eye on the gas gauge and stopped where he felt safe. "It was frightening traveling through the South, it was."[83] Tom Harbut, Will Harbut's son, who co-owned and trained Touch Bar for the 1962 Kentucky Derby, remembered the track kitchen at Keeneland. "I think we all went in the same door and as soon as we got in that door we had to go in this door (to the left) and the whites went in that door (to the right). Then we'd all come out the same door and go back to the same barn. I often wonder, what's going through a white man's mind when that happens."[84] It was a question Isaac Murphy might have asked. It was a question about why racism exists and why it endures.

A few Black horsemen managed to reach the top level of the sport, like Oscar Dishman, who trained Silver Series on the Kentucky Derby trail in 1977 and worked him to win the American Derby that year, a result that recalled Murphy's great winning streak of the 1880s.[85] Dishman won stakes races and elite handicaps, but he knew he missed chances at top-class horses, because so much of training depended on the kind of personal connections with owners, chats over drinks and lunches, that de jure and de facto segregation made exponentially harder.[86] Hank Allen, after a career in Major League Baseball with his brother, superstar Dick Allen, moved on to training horses and saddled Northern Wolf for the Kentucky Derby in 1989. He found himself confronted with questions about why so few Black men trained and rode at the highest level and actually had to explain it wasn't because all Black men were too large and muscle-bound to be jockeys. It was a matter of opportunity, of being given a shot at promotion to prestigious jobs, a chance to work with the best horses. Allen pointed to jockey Wayne Barnett, who had ridden a horse for him in the Preakness in 1985. "When they thought he was . . . from Panama, he got plenty of rides. . . . But when they found out he was from Detroit, all of a sudden he couldn't get any mounts. You tell me why."[87] (In 2016, Barnett returned to the saddle after decades away and became the leading rider at Hazel Park in Detroit.)[88]

In the twenty-first century, remembering Isaac Murphy has taken new forms. In Lexington, civic activists constructed a memorial art garden on the site of his final home. Archaeologists laid bare the house's foundations, alongside markers celebrating his career. But memorializing Murphy is only part of efforts to celebrate the East End, the area in which he and his friends and family made their lives. The neighborhood theater, the Lyric, where Count Basie played, has been remodeled and hosts community events.[89] Local historic preservation organizations sponsor tours that tell the stories of Black professionals in town, including those who worked at the track. The cemetery in which Lucy Murphy rests, along with more than 150 African American horsemen, is carefully maintained and the stories of the dead honored. Murphy himself is still memorialized at the Horse Park, though the front of the marker now holds a quote from Murphy himself in place of the original epitaph: "I am as proud of my calling as I am of my record and I believe my life will be recorded a success, though the reputation I enjoy was earned in the stable and in the saddle."

In 2020, as Louisville prepared for an unprecedented September Kentucky Derby, rescheduled during the COVID-19 pandemic, the city roiled with protests over violence against Black people, including the death of Breonna Taylor, shot by local police executing a no-knock warrant. Once again, activists debated disrupting the Derby, this time to call attention to the systemic racism that the civil rights movement of the 1960s had left still ossified. And they began pressuring Greg Harbut, Tom Harbut's grandson, who owned a Derby entry, Necker Island, with businessman Ray Daniels.

To run Necker Island in the Derby was to oppose the protests, activists insisted. Harbut quietly but firmly explained that he believed in the protests and adamantly supported justice for Breonna Taylor. But racing was not like basketball, where African American athletes had forced significant discussion about racial justice that summer by their boycotts of games. It was not the absence of Black men in a prominent position at the Kentucky Derby that would be noted, but their presence. Harbut and Daniels wanted to represent and celebrate generations of Black men too often erased. When Tom Harbut had brought Touch Bar to the 1962 Kentucky Derby, he wasn't allowed to sit in the grandstand. Now his grandson ceremonially walked with his horse to the paddock.[90] In that walk, he was telling a story that stretched back for centuries, a story of Black men's labor and love and their efforts to make a living and a life.

Black people who work at all levels of racing recognize that, as African American industry executive Jason Wilson summed up, "I do not see a lot of people that look like me." "When I run horses, I'm the only Black in the shed, the only Black on the end of the shank. . . . It's sad, but it's true," groom Jerry Dixon, Sr., a third-generation horseman, shrugged grimly in an interview in 2022, idly patting the white-blazed chestnut colt beside him.[91] But with effort and thought, that could change. Harbut and Daniels are seeking to build syndicates to bring more African American owners into racing, as are a number of other groups. Their Ed Brown Society provides scholarships and internship opportunities to young Black men and women interested in working in the industry.[92] As these efforts continue, Isaac Murphy may take his place, not as a cardboard cutout to be celebrated in isolation from his community and his history, but as one of a long line of Black horsemen and Black athletes who have played their part in the struggle for Black citizenship in America.

In the summer of 2020, jockeys took a knee on the first day of racing at Belmont Park in solidarity with civil rights protestors. Louisiana-born Kendrick Carmouche, a second-generation African American rider, helped organize the gesture.[93] In 2021, Carmouche piloted Wood Memorial winner Bourbonic in the Kentucky Derby. And a few days after Jerry Dixon lamented how few Black men were still in the barns, Rich Strike, the horse who'd patiently stood beside him during his interview, came home an 80-to-1 winner in the 2022 Kentucky Derby. Dixon and his son, fourth-generation horseman Jerry Dixon, Jr., led the winner off in triumph. Almost a hundred and fifty years since Isaac Murphy won his last Kentucky Derby, Black men are still showing off the skills that made him world famous, in a sport that lets us see poignant and painful truths about our nation, about what we love and what we believe. "It's really," reflected African American horseman Howard Amos, "a very beautiful game."[94]

NOTES

———

Introduction

1. "More Records Dashed," *Anaconda Standard* 29 August 1890, 2.

2. Ralph Ellison, *Three Days Before the Shooting,* ed. John F. Callahan and Adam Bradley (New York: Modern Library, 2010), 935.

CHAPTER 1. "Reputable and Entitled to Credit"

1. Jerry Burns records, Application WC137891, Pension #174318, Case Files of Approved Pension Applications of Widows and Other Veterans of the Army and Navy Who Served Mainly in the Civil War and the War with Spain, National Archives, Record Group 15, Accessed Fold3.com.

2. America Burns account card, Record #1479, 21 April 1873, U.S. Freedman's Bank Records, 1865–1874, Roll 11, Lexington, Kentucky, Accessed Ancestry.com; Aaron Astor, *Rebels on the Border: Civil War, Emancipation, and the Reconstruction of Kentucky and Missouri* (Baton Rouge: Louisiana State University Press, 2012), 21–27.

3. Population schedules, Clark County, Kentucky, 1850 and 1860 U.S. Census; Slave schedules, Clark County, Kentucky, 1860 U.S. Census; Clark County tax lists, 1852–1858, Kentucky Historical Society.

4. America Burns account card, Record #1479, U.S. Freedman's Bank Records, Accessed Ancestry.com; Jerry Skillman, compiled service record, 114th U.S. Colored Infantry, Record Group 94, Roll RG94-USCT-114-Bx49 National Archives, Accessed Fold3.com. Jerry Burns's enlistment and service records are filed under the name Jerry Skillman. Population schedules, Bourbon County, Kentucky, 1860 U.S. Census. The Bourbon County Tanners share multiple proper names with the Clark County Tanners.

5. Jerry Burns records, Case Files Approved Pension Applications, Pension #174318, Accessed Fold3.com.

6. Tera W. Hunter, *Bound in Wedlock: Slave and Free Black Marriage in the Nineteenth Century* (Cambridge, MA: Harvard University Press, 2017), 33, 54–59.

7. Jerry Burns records, Case Files Approved Pension Applications, Pension #174318, Accessed Fold3.com; Population Schedule, Bourbon County, Kentucky, 1860 U.S. Census; Birth Records, Clark County, Kentucky, 1861, Accessed Ancestry.com.

8. Henry Cleveland, *Alexander H. Stephens in Public and Private* (Philadelphia: National Publishing, 1866), 721.

9. Astor, *Rebels on the Border*, 87, 101.

10. Victor B. Howard, "The Civil War in Kentucky: The Slave Claims His Freedom," *Journal of Negro History* 67, no. 3 (1982): 250; Victor B. Howard, *Black Liberation in Kentucky* (Lexington: University Press of Kentucky, 1983), 34–35; Marion B. Lucas, *A History of Blacks in Kentucky* vol. 1 (Frankfort: Kentucky Historical Society, 1982), 153–54; Astor, *Rebels on the Border*, 127–28.

11. Jerry Skillman, compiled service record, 114th U.S. Colored Infantry, Accessed Fold3.com; C. C. Skillman, U.S. Civil War Draft Registration Records, 1863–1865, Accessed Ancestry.com.

12. Helen H. LaCroix, "In the Absence of Reconstruction: Race, Politics, and State Power in Kentucky, 1850–1872," PhD diss., University of Wisconsin, 2011, 103; Astor, *Rebels on the Border*, 133–34.

13. Astor, *Rebels on the Border*, 126; LaCroix, "In the Absence of Reconstruction," 100.

14. Elijah P. Marrs, *Life and History of the Rev. Elijah P. Marrs, First Pastor of Bluegrass Baptist Church and Author* (Louisville: Bradley and Gilbert, 1885), 22.

15. Jerry Skillman, compiled service record, 114th U.S. Colored Infantry, Accessed Fold3.com; Jerry Burns records, Case Files Approved Pension Applications, Pension #174318, Accessed Fold3.com.

16. LaCroix, "In the Absence of Reconstruction," 105–8.

17. Howard, *Black Liberation*, 79–84; LaCroix, "In the Absence of Reconstruction," 113–20; Ross A. Webb, *Kentucky in the Reconstruction Era* (Lexington: University Press of Kentucky, 1979), 38–39.

18. Patrick A. Lewis, *For Slavery and Union: Benjamin Buckner and Kentucky Loyalists in the Civil War* (Lexington: University Press of Kentucky, 2015), 165–66; John Kellogg, "The Formation of Black Residential Areas in Lexington, Kentucky, 1865–1887," *Journal of Southern History* 48, no. 1 (1982): 30; Howard, *Black Liberation*, 100; Astor, *Rebels on the Border*, 165.

19. Lucas, *Blacks in Kentucky*, 196, 274–75; Kellogg, "Formation of Black Residential Areas," 33–51.

20. Webb, *Kentucky in the Reconstruction Era*, 44–50.

21. Stephen Burbridge to Edwin M. Stanton, 20 July 1865, Edwin M. Stanton Papers, Library of Congress, https://www.loc.gov/item/mss41202028/.

22. George C. Wright, *Racial Violence in Kentucky, 1865–1900* (Baton Rouge: Louisiana State University Press, 1990), 41; LaCroix, "In the Absence of Reconstruction," 159; Astor, *Rebels on the Border*, 138–39; Lewis, *For Slavery and Union*, 160.

23. Tera W. Hunter, *To 'Joy My Freedom: Southern Black Women's Lives and Labors After the Civil War* (Cambridge, MA: Harvard University Press, 1997), 26, 52–58.

24. Jerry Burns records, Case Files Approved Pension Applications, Pension #174318, Accessed Fold3.com.

25. Deed Book 49, Fayette County Clerk's Office, 89–90; America Burns account card, Record #1479, U.S. Freedman's Bank Records, Accessed Ancestry.com; Fayette County Tax Lists, 1870, Kentucky Historical Society.

26. Population schedule, Fayette County, Kentucky, 1870 U.S. Census.

27. America Burns account cards, Record #294, 28 December 1870, and Record #1479, 21 April 1873, U.S. Freedman's Bank Records, Accessed Ancestry.com; Webb, *Kentucky in the Reconstruction Era*, 53; Lucas, *Blacks in Kentucky*, 283.

28. James Murphy account card, Record #1273, 26 October 1872, U.S. Freedman's Bank Records, Accessed Ancestry.com.

29. Population schedule, Fayette County, Kentucky, 1870 U.S. Census.

30. Webb, *Kentucky in the Reconstruction Era*, 56; Astor, *Rebels on the Border*, 147–48; Lucas, *Blacks in Kentucky*, 234–40; Wright, *Racial Violence in Kentucky*, 37–38.

31. *Proceedings of the First Convention of Colored Men of Kentucky, Held in Lexington, March the 22d, 23d, 24th and 26th, 1866* (Louisville: Civil & Calvert, 1866), 24–25, https://omeka.coloredconventions.org/items/show/459.

32. Victor B. Howard, "The Black Testimony Controversy in Kentucky, 1866–1872," *Journal of Negro History* 58, no. 2 (1973): 154–55; Astor, *Rebels on the Border*, 158.

33. Astor, *Rebels on the Border*, 184–85.

34. "Memorial of a Committee Appointed at a Meeting of Colored Citizens of Frankfort, Ky., and Vicinity," 11 April 1871, Senate Misc. Documents, No. 49, 42nd Congress, 1st Session, https://omeka.coloredconventions.org/items/show/539.

35. Webb, *Kentucky in the Reconstruction Era,* 57.

36. Howard, "Black Testimony Controversy in Kentucky," 162–63.

37. LaCroix, "In the Absence of Reconstruction," 217–19.

38. Howard, "Black Testimony Controversy in Kentucky," 164.

39. Robert M. Goldman, *Reconstruction and Black Suffrage: Losing the Vote in Reese and* Cruikshank (Lawrence: University Press of Kansas, 2001), 243–44, 282–84; LaCroix, "In the Absence of Reconstruction," 222–35.

40. Patrick A. Lewis, "The Democratic Partisan Militia and the Black Peril: The Kentucky Militia, Racial Violence, and the Fifteenth Amendment, 1870–1873," *Civil War History* 56, no. 2 (2010): 152; Astor, *Rebels on the Border,* 222–23; LaCroix, "In the Absence of Reconstruction," 181.

41. Goldman, *Reconstruction and Black Suffrage,* 65–66.

42. Lewis, *For Slavery and Union,* 166–70.

43. Lewis, *For Slavery and Union,* 166–67, 180; Goldman, *Reconstruction and Black Suffrage,* 66–67.

44. Lewis, *For Slavery and Union,* 182–84; Goldman, *Reconstruction and Black Suffrage,* 368–70.

45. LaCroix, "In the Absence of Reconstruction," 178; Goldman, *Reconstruction and Black Suffrage,* 64.

46. Peyton Harrison Hoge, *Moses Drury Hoge: His Life and Letters* (Richmond: Presbyterian Committee of Publication, 1899), 445.

47. Population schedule, Fayette County, Kentucky, 1870 U.S. Census.

48. Hunter, *Bound in Wedlock,* 278.

49. *Simon Williams vs. America Burns,* Box 191, Drawer No. 1684–86, Fayette County Circuit Court Records, Kentucky Department of Libraries and Archives.

50. Deed Book 54, Fayette County Clerk's Office, 598–99.

51. America Burns account card, Record #1479, U.S. Freedman's Bank Records, Accessed Ancestry.com; Jerry Burns records, Case Files Approved Pension Applications, Pension #174318, Accessed Fold3.com.

52. "Ike, the Black Archer," *St. Louis Post Dispatch* 12 June 1889, 10; Jerry Burns records, Case Files Approved Pension Applications, Pension #174318, Accessed Fold3.com; America Burns account card, Record #294, U.S. Freedman's Bank Records, Accessed Ancestry.com; Population schedule, Fayette County, Kentucky, 1870 U.S. Census.

53. "Ike Murphy's Real Name," *Chicago Inter Ocean* 28 July 1891, 3; *Prather's Lexington City Directory for 1875 and 1876* (Lexington: Transylvania Printing), 132.

54. L. P. Tarlton, "Isaac Murphy: A Memorial," *Thoroughbred Record* 21 March 1896, 136.

55. "The Turf," *New York Sportsman* 4 April 1885, 260.

56. "Bitten by a Horse," *Turf, Field and Farm* 26 April 1878, 262.

57. "Killed on the Race Track," *New York Sportsman* 14 July 1877, 22.

58. John H. Davis, *The American Turf* (New York: John Polhemus, 1907), 86.

59. Davis, *The American Turf*, 86–88.

60. Hamilton Busbey, "The Running Turf in America," *Harper's* July 1870, 254.

61. J. Michael Rhyne, "'Conduct . . . Inexcusable and Unjustifiable': Bound Children, Battered Freedwomen, and the Limits of Emancipation," *Journal of Southern History* 42, no. 2 (2008): 324.

62. Tarlton, "A Memorial," 136.

63. Tarlton, "A Memorial," 136.

64. Walter S. Vosburgh, *Racing in America, 1866–1921* (New York: Jockey Club, 1922), 57.

65. Busbey, "The Running Turf in America," 251.

66. Maryjean Wall, *How Kentucky Became Southern* (Lexington: University Press of Kentucky, 2010), 39.

67. Anita Leslie, *The Remarkable Mr. Jerome* (New York: Henry Holt and Company, 1954), 78; William H. P. Robertson, *The History of Thoroughbred Racing in America* (Englewood Cliffs, NJ: Prentice Hall, 1964), 103–4; Vosburgh, *Racing in America*, 5–6.

68. Joe H. Palmer, *This Was Racing*, ed. Red Smith (New York: A. S. Barnes, 1953), 211–12.

69. Eric Homberger, *Mrs. Astor's New York: Money and Social Power in a Gilded Age* (New Haven: Yale University Press, 2002), 182; Busbey, "The Running Turf in America," 251.

70. "The American Jockey Club," *Spirit of the Times* 8 September 1866, 25.

71. "Our New York Letter," *Kentucky Live Stock Record* 4 August 1877, 65; "The Great Strike," *Spirit of the Times* 4 August 1877, 750.

72. "The Labor in Central Kentucky," *Turf, Field and Farm* 10 August 1878, 89.

73. Robertson, *History of Thoroughbred Racing*, 105–6; Vosburgh, *Racing in America*, 26–27.

74. Lyman Horace Weeks, *The American Turf* (New York: Historical Company, 1898), 45–46.

75. "The Louisville Jockey Club," *Turf, Field and Farm* 10 July 1874, 28.

76. William Walker, death certificate, 20 September 1933, Accessed Ancestry .com; *American Racing Calendar of 1876* (New York: Turf, Field and Farm, 1876), 76, 80; Ben H. Weaver, "The Passing of 'Uncle Bill,'" *Turf and Sport Digest* December 1933, 39; *New York Sportsman* 21 July 1877, 35.

77. "An Interview with F. B. Harper—Some Inconsistencies Worth Noting," *Kentucky Live Stock Record* 3 August 1878, 72–73.

78. *Prather's Lexington City Directory for 1875 and 1876*, 49, 245, 144; John T. Clay, death certificate, 24 March 1934, Accessed Ancestry.com; "In the World of Sports," *Indianapolis Freeman* 11 November 1905, 6; "Blue-Grass Flyers," *Cincinnati Enquirer* 20 April 1878, 6.

79. "Horses in Training in Kentucky," *Kentucky Live Stock Record* 23 March 1878, 179; "Horses in Training in Kentucky," *Kentucky Live Stock Record* 1 March 1879, 131; "Race Horses in Training," *Turf, Field and Farm,* 4 February 1881, 69.

80. Dudley Allen, compiled service record, 5th U.S. Colored Cavalry, Record Group 94, National Archives, Accessed Fold3.com; "Horses in Training," *Kentucky Live Stock Record* 26 February 1875, 55; "Horses in Training in Kentucky for the Spring Campaign," *Kentucky Live Stock Record* 17 February 1877, 101.

81. "Ike, the Black Archer," 10; "The Inaugural of the Louisville Jockey Club," *Kentucky Live Stock Record* 21 May 1875, 242.

82. Tarlton, "A Memorial,"136; "The Kentucky Association," *Kentucky Live Stock Record,* 23 September 1876, 196. Murphy himself claimed he'd won on Glentina at the small Crab Orchard track before that first recorded win. See "Isaac Murphy," *Lexington Leader* 20 March 1889, 3.

83. "Louisville Jockey Club," *Kentucky Live Stock Record* 30 September 1876, 210–11; "The Louisville Races," *New York Sportsman* 30 September 1876, 470.

84. "Ike, the Black Archer," 10; *Krik's Guide to the Turf, Part 1: Record of the Races Run in the United States in 1877* (New York: H. G. Crickmore, 1878), 47, 105, 108, 135, 138–39, 165.

85. "Horse Gossip—Sale of a Racing Interest," *Turf, Field and Farm* 20 April 1877, 249; "Stock Gossip," *Kentucky Live Stock Record* 22 December 1877, 388; Franklin County Tax Lists, 1875, Kentucky Historical Society.

86. "Kentucky Association Races," *Turf, Field and Farm* 21 September 1878, 179.

87. Robertson, *History of Thoroughbred Racing,* 127–30, 194.

88. "Sale of Spendthrift and Miser," *Kentucky Live Stock Record* 4 January 1879, 9.

89. Edward L. Bowen, *Legacies of the Turf* (Lexington: Blood-Horse, 2003), 9–12; Dan M. Bowmar, *Giants of the Turf* (Lexington: Blood-Horse, 1960), 103–25; Heather Cox Richardson, *West from Appomattox: The Reconstruction of America After the Civil War* (New Haven: Yale University Press, 2007), 131.

90. Edwin Lefevre, "James Robert Keene," *Cosmopolitan Magazine* November 1902, 93.

91. "Track Talk," *Chicago Tribune* 21 December 1879, 7.

92. "Horse Notes," *New Orleans Daily Democrat* 6 June 1879, 10.

93. "Stock Gossip," *Kentucky Live Stock Record* 14 June 1879, 375.

94. W. S. Vosburgh, *Cherry and Black: The Career of Mr. Pierre Lorillard on the Turf* (New York: privately printed, 1916), 68.

95. "Saratoga," *Spirit of the Times* 26 July 1879, 624.

96. "Saratoga," *Spirit of the Times* 16 August 1879, 35–36.

97. "Falsetto, the Great Three-Year-Old," *Spirit of the Times* 23 August 1879, 57.

98. "Falsetto, the Great Three-Year-Old," 57; "Falsetto," *Kentucky Live Stock Record* 20 July 1904, 71.

99. *New York Sportsman* 31 January 1880, 51.

100. Mortality Schedule, Fayette County, Kentucky, 1880 U.S. Census, Accessed Ancestry.com. The record of her death, which must have been compiled with data gathered from a medical professional or a city official, lists her as forty-nine, but she personally told both the pension office and the bank that she was ten years younger.

101. "Ike, The Black Archer," 10.

102. Tarlton, "A Memorial," 136.

103. America Burns account card, Record #1479, U.S. Freedman's Bank Records, Accessed Ancestry.com.

CHAPTER 2. "He Had Famous Flyers to Ride Then"

1. "Breeding Farms in Kentucky," *Kentucky Live Stock Record* 28 February 1885, 136; Population schedule, Franklin County, Kentucky, 1880 U.S. Census.

2. "Horse Notes from Lexington," *Turf, Field and Farm* 26 February 1886, 159.

3. "Old Kentucky Route," *Kentucky Live Stock Record* 6 July 1889, 15.

4. William Woodward, *Memoir of Andrew Jackson, Africanus* (New York: Derrydale, 1938), 16.

5. "More Turf Stars for the Races," *St. Louis Globe Democrat* 9 June 1884, 3.

6. "Saratoga Letter," *New York Globe* 18 August 1883, 4; *Kirwin & Co.'s Saratoga Springs Directory, 1884* (Saratoga Springs: Wm. H. Kirwin, 1884), 134; Myra B. Young Armstead, *Lord, Please Don't Take Me in August: African Americans in Newport and Saratoga Springs, 1870–1930* (Urbana: University of Illinois Press, 1999), 58.

7. "The Kentucky University," *New York Freeman* 29 May 1886, 1; *Caron's Directory of the City of Louisville for 1885* (Louisville: Caron, 1885), 827.

8. "Isaac Murphy," *Lexington Leader* 20 March 1889, 3; "Sporting World,"

Cincinnati Enquirer 23 September 1883, 10; "Tips from the Racetrack," *New Orleans Picayune* 25 September 1883, 2.

9. "Isaac Murphy," 3.

10. *Krik's Guide to the Turf, Part 1: Record of the Races Run in the United States in 1877* (New York: H. G. Crickmore, 1878), 25–28; *Krik's Guide to the Turf, Part 1* (New York: H. G. Crickmore, 1883), xxxiii–xxxvi; *Goodwin's Annual Turf Guide for 1882* (New York: Goodwin Brothers, 1883), unpaginated; "The Racing Weights," *New York Sportsman* 13 November 1875, 294; "Horse Gossip," *Turf, Field and Farm* 18 November 1881, 326; "New Weights of the Louisville Jockey Club," *Kentucky Live Stock Record* 10 October 1881, 377.

11. "Jockeys—'Heavy Weight Versus Light,'" *Turf, Field and Farm* 7 May 1886, 375; "Turf Reform and Raising the Weights," *Turf, Field and Farm* 3 December 1886, 484.

12. Christopher Poole, "Cauthen's Agony No Real Surprise," *London Standard* 13 December 1985, 47.

13. *Krik's Guide to the Turf, Part 1* (New York: H. G. Crickmore, 1879), xiv–xvi; "Saratoga," *Spirit of the Times* 26 July 1879, 624.

14. "The Turf," *New York Sportsman* 30 June 1883, 512; "Turf Notes," *Nashville Banner* 2 July 1883, 3.

15. "Turf Notes," *Nashville Daily American* 13 March 1883, 2.

16. "A Jockey's Life," *Chicago Tribune* 10 July 1885, 2; "How a Jockey Lives," *Frank Leslie's Illustrated Newspaper* 22 August 1885, 14; Jimmy Breslin, *Sunny Jim: The Life of America's Most Beloved Horseman* (Garden City, NY: Doubleday and Co., 1962), 130–31.

17. "The Metropolitan Meeting," *Spirit of the Times* 15 October 1881, 303.

18. Hugh McIlvanney, *McIlvanney on Horseracing* (Edinburgh: Mainstream, 1997), 70–71.

19. "Interesting Racing Clippings," *New Orleans Picayune* 19 February 1889, 2; "Racing," *Buffalo Courier* 18 February 1889, 3.

20. "Isaac Murphy's Finest Finish," *New York Age* 21 June 1890, 2.

21. T. Thomas Fortune, "The Prince of Jockeys," *New York Age* 5 July 1890, 1.

22. "Saratoga Gossip," *Spirit of the Times* 9 August 1879, 1–2; "The P.Q. Turf Club Races," *Montreal Gazette* 25 June 1889, 8.

23. "Death of J. W. Hunt Reynolds," *Kentucky Live Stock Record* 25 September 1880, 200.

24. "Horse Gossip," *Turf, Field and Farm* 19 November 1880, 326; "Frankfort," *Turf, Field and Farm* 18 February 1881, 103; "Stock Gossip," *Kentucky Live Stock Record* 28 January 1882, 53.

25. "The Louisville Spring Meeting," *Kentucky Live Stock Record* 4 June 1881, 361.

26. "Horse Gossip," *Turf, Field and Farm* 24 November 1882, 347; "Horses in Training," *Kentucky Live Stock Record* 18 March 1882, 164–65.

27. "Louisville (Ky.) Races," *Turf, Field and Farm* 21 May 1880, 324–25; *Krik's Guide to the Turf, Part 1* (New York: H. G. Crickmore, 1880), 25.

28. "St. Louis Jockey Club," *Kentucky Live Stock Record* 10 June 1882, 355–56; "First Meeting of the Saratoga Racing Association," *Turf, Field and Farm* 21 July 1882, 37–38; "Louisville Jockey Club," *Kentucky Live Stock Record* 2 June 1883, 338–41; "Latonia Jockey Club," *Kentucky Live Stock Record* 16 June 1883, 372–74; "Chicago Driving Park," *Kentucky Live Stock Record* 7 July 1883, 3–5.

29. *Goodwin's Guide 1882*, unpaginated; "Isaac Murphy, Colored Jockey," *New York Sportsman* 20 January 1883, 33–34.

30. *Goodwin's Annual Turf Guide for 1883* (New York: Goodwin Brothers, 1883), lvii.

31. *Krik's Guide to the Turf, Part 1, 1882*, xxviii.

32. "Horse Gossip," *Turf, Field and Farm* 7 March 1879, 150.

33. Walter S. Vosburgh, *Racing in America, 1866–1921* (New York: Jockey Club, 1922), 107.

34. "First Summer Meeting," *Spirit of the Times* 26 July 1879, 625; "Long Branch," *Spirit of the Times* 16 July 1881, 645; "Saratoga," *Spirit of the Times* 30 July 1881, 715; "Checkmate," *Turf, Field and Farm* 12 August 1881, 102; "Saratoga (N.Y.) Races—Annual Meeting," *Turf, Field and Farm* 19 August 1881, 113–14; "American Jockey Club Races," *Turf, Field and Farm* 14 October 1881, 241.

35. "Hindoo and Checkmate," *Brooklyn Eagle* 21 May 1882, 3.

36. "General Kentucky News," *Louisville Courier Journal* 4 September 1883, 4.

37. "Stock Gossip," *Kentucky Live Stock Record* 17 March 1883, 166; "Post and Paddock," *Spirit of the Times* 24 March 1883, 206.

38. Records for Osborn's birthdate and age differ wildly. The 1870 census lists her as twenty-two and Lucy as five. In 1880, the census recorded her as ten years older than her daughter; on her death certificate, she is listed as only four years older.

39. Lucy B. Murphy, death certificate, 26 February 1910, Accessed Ancestry .com; Population schedules, Franklin County, Kentucky, 1870 and 1880 U.S. Census.

40. "Frankfort," *Louisville Courier Journal* 25 January 1883, 5; "A Jockey's Wedding," *Nashville Daily American* 27 January 1883, 5.

41. Her death certificate lists her birthday as January 4. It also lists her birth year as 1868, which would make her fifteen when they married and conflicts with

both the 1870 and 1880 censuses, which suggest a birth year of 1865. A marriage closely following her eighteenth birthday seems a reasonable possibility.

42. Tera W. Hunter, *Bound in Wedlock: Slave and Free Black Marriage in the Nineteenth Century* (Cambridge, MA: Harvard University Press, 2017), 293–96.

43. "Ike, the Black Archer," *St. Louis Post Dispatch* 12 June 1889, 10.

44. Deed Book 68, Fayette County Clerk's Office, 453–54.

45. "Horse Jottings from Many Sources," *New Orleans Picayune* 7 December 1883, 8; "Turf Talk," *Nashville Daily American* 17 December 1883, 2.

46. *Spirit of the Times* 15 December 1883, 590; "The Fees of Jockeys," *New York Sportsman* 17 March 1883, 174; "In Re Jockey's Fees," *New York Sportsman* 31 March 1883, 217.

47. "Corrigan's Rise to Fame," *Kansas City Star* 15 January 1905, 11.

48. "Difficulty of Mr. E. Corrigan at West Side Park," *Kentucky Live Stock Record* 28 July 1888, 52; "Horse Gossip," *Turf, Field and Farm* 3 August 1888, 105; "Saratoga," *Spirit of the Times* 28 July 1888, 6; "Ed. Corrigan as Seen by New York Eyes," *Kansas City Star* 11 March 1889, 2.

49. "Horse Gossip," *Turf, Field and Farm* 6 January 1888, 12; "Edwin Corrigan Attacks Thomas A. Mosier," *Kentucky Live Stock Record* 12 November 1887, 310–11; "E. Corrigan's Attack on Dr. Morrison Munford," *Kentucky Live Stock Record* 17 December 1887, 393.

50. "The Alleged Charges Against Mr. E. Corrigan," *New York Sportsman* 1 December 1883, 421; "Post and Paddock," *Spirit of the Times* 2 May 1885, 418.

51. "Louisville Jockey Club," *Spirit of the Times* 24 May 1884, 322–25.

52. "William Bird, Trainer for Gov. Bowie," *New York Sportsman* 4 August 1883, 120; "Post and Paddock," *Spirit of the Times* 5 July 1884, 715.

53. "Latonia Fall Meeting," *Kentucky Live Stock Record* 22 Sept. 1883, 180–82.

54. "The Running Turf," *Louisville Courier Journal* 11 May 1884, 12; "The Honors of the Turf," *New York Times* 17 May 1884, 2.

55. "Louisville," *Spirit of the Times* 24 May 1884, 516; "The Lexington Meeting," *Louisville Courier Journal* 16 May 1884, 6; "Louisville Jockey Club," *Kentucky Live Stock Record* 24 May 1884, 322–25; "Louisville Jockey Club," *Kentucky Live Stock Record* 31 May 1884, 338–40; "'Climax' at Louisville," *New York Sportsman* 24 May 1884, 400.

56. "Spring Meeting of the Louisville Jockey Club, Louisville, Ky.," *Turf, Field and Farm* 23 May 1884, 404–5; *Goodwin's Annual Turf Guide for 1884* (New York: Goodwin Brothers, 1884), 52.

57. "Washington Park Club," *Kentucky Live Stock Record* 28 June 1884, 408.

58. Gerald R. Gems, *The Windy City Wars: Labor, Leisure, and Sport in the Making of Chicago* (Lanham, MD: Scarecrow Press, 1997), 33; Steven A. Riess,

Horse Racing the Chicago Way: Gambling, Politics, and Organized Crime, 1837–1911 (Syracuse: Syracuse University Press, 2022), 50–51.

59. Charles E. Trevathan, *The American Thoroughbred* (New York: Macmillan, 1905), 413.

60. "The Inauguration of the Washington Park Club," *Kentucky Live Stock Record* 5 July 1884, 3–4; "Washington Park," *Spirit of the Times* 5 July 1884, 710.

61. *Goodwin's Official Annual Turf Guide for 1885* (New York: Goodwin Brothers, 1885), lxxv.

62. "Chicago," *Spirit of the Times* 4 July 1885, 714; "The Chicago Derby," *Spirit of the Times* 11 July 1885, 744; "Our Chicago Letter," *Turf, Field and Farm* 3 July 1885, 4.

63. "Blue Grass Notes," *Spirit of the Times* 25 July 1885, 815.

64. "Saratoga Races," *Turf, Field and Farm* 31 July 1885, 90.

65. Vosburgh, *Racing in America*, 124–25.

66. Lyman Horace Weeks, *The American Turf* (New York: Historical Company, 1898), 100.

67. "The Kansas City Stable," *Turf, Field and Farm* 6 November 1885, 377.

68. "Isaac Murphy," 3.

69. "The Defeat of Freeland," *New York Tribune* 21 August 1885, 4.

70. Kent Hollingsworth, *The Great Ones* (Lexington: Blood-Horse, 1970), 189–91.

71. "Freeland Supreme," *New York Herald* 19 August 1885, 6; *Goodwin's Guide 1885*, 191.

72. "Racing Past and to Come," *Turf, Field and Farm* 21 August 1885, 147.

73. "Saratoga," *Spirit of the Times* 29 August 1885, 146–47.

74. "Beaten by a Head," *Kansas City Times* 21 August 1885, 1; "Monmouth Park," *Spirit of the Times* 29 August 1885, 137.

75. "The East Wins the Match," *New York Tribune* 25 August 1885, 2.

76. "Post and Paddock," *Spirit of the Times* 29 August 1885, 151.

77. "The Defeat of Freeland," 4.

78. Hollingsworth, *Great Ones*, 190.

79. "Notes of the Turf," *New York Times* 14 September 1885, 2.

80. "The Turf," *New Orleans Picayune* 15 September 1885, 8.

81. "Principal Winning Jockeys," *Spirit of the Times* 26 September 1885, 280.

82. "The Spirit Picture Gallery," *Spirit of the Times* 29 August 1885, 144; "Spirit of the Times," *Spirit of the Times* 26 September 1885, 284.

83. "Saratoga," *Spirit of the Times* 5 September 1885, 169–70; "Erratic Race Horses," *Kansas City Times* 12 October 1885, 2; "Echoes of the Day," *New York*

Sportsman 17 October 1885, 314; "Sporting Gossip," *Kansas City Times* 19 October 1885, 2.

84. "Isaac Murphy, Jockey," *San Francisco Examiner* 31 March 1886, 2; "Echoes of the Day," *New York Sportsman* 3 April 1886, 246; "Points for Turfmen," *Chicago Inter Ocean* 4 April 1886, 4; "The Tattler's Tattle," *New York Sportsman* 8 May 1886, 351.

85. "Pacific Coast Races," *Arizona Star* 15 April 1886, 2.

86. Weeks, *American Turf,* 49; C. B. Glasscock, *Lucky Baldwin* (Indianapolis: Bobbs-Merrill, 1933), 174.

87. Glasscock, *Lucky Baldwin,* 237–38; Hubert Howe Bancroft, *Chronicles of the Builders of the Commonwealth* vol. 3 (San Francisco: History Company, 1892), 352–53.

88. Debra Ginsburg, "Lucky Baldwin's Racing School," *Thoroughbred of California* June 1994, 38–46.

89. John Dizikes, *Yankee Doodle Dandy: The Life and Times of Tod Sloan* (New Haven: Yale University Press, 2000), 49.

90. Bancroft, *Chronicles of the Builders,* 365.

91. "Verona Baldwin," *Los Angeles Herald* 31 March 1887, 3.

92. *Tampa Tribune* 19 March 1911, 20; "Her Mind Astray, Said Judge Slack," *San Francisco Examiner* 17 September 1896, 9.

93. "Memphis," *Spirit of the Times* 25 April 1891, 609–10.

94. *Goodwin's Official Annual Turf Guide for 1886* (New York: Goodwin Brothers, 1886), 33.

95. *Goodwin's Guide 1886,* 88, 229, 233, 276, 398.

96. "Monmouth Park Association," *Kentucky Live Stock Record* 14 August 1886, 99.

97. "Murphy and Volante," *Chicago Inter Ocean* 20 July 1886, 2.

98. "Chicago," *Spirit of the Times* 3 July 1886, 722–23.

99. "Murphy and Volante," 2.

100. "Isaac Murphy," 3.

101. "Post and Paddock," *Spirit of the Times* 27 August 1887, 163.

102. Hollingsworth, *Great Ones,* 98; *Goodwin's Official Annual Turf Guide for 1887* (New York: Goodwin Brothers, 1888), 181, 184, 220, 225, 277, 322, 350, 382, 411, 416, 465.

103. "Racing at Chicago," *Turf, Field and Farm* 15 July 1887, 52; "Saratoga Races," *Turf, Field and Farm* 26 August 1887, 180–81.

104. *Goodwin's Official Annual Turf Guide for 1888* (New York: Goodwin Brothers, 1888), 73, 113–14, 148, 152, 182.

105. *Goodwin's Guide 1888,* 203.

106. "Chicago's Meeting," *New York Sportsman* 30 June 1888, 626; "Emperor of Norfolk's Derby," *New York Herald* 24 June 1888, 12.

107. "The Meeting at Washington Park," *Turf, Field and Farm* 13 July 1888, 35; *Goodwin's Guide 1888*, 226–27, 230.

108. "Isaac Murphy," 3.

109. "E. J. Baldwin's Norfolk Is Dead," *San Francisco Chronicle* 16 December 1907, 7.

110. Julian Wilson, *100 Greatest Racehorses* (London: Queen Anne Press, 1987), 85–86; Roger Mortimer, *Twenty Great Horses* (London: Cassell, 1967), 59–64.

111. "Three Colored Sports," *Chicago Tribune* 10 July 1887, 17.

112. John Welcome, *Fred Archer: A Complete Study* (London: Lambourn, 1990), 74.

113. "IROQUOIS: American Captures the Epsom Derby!," *Spirit of the Times* 4 June 1881, 462; Walter S. Vosburgh, *Cherry and Black: The Career of Mr. Pierre Lorillard on the Turf* (New York: Privately printed, 1916), 43–44.

114. Welcome, *Fred Archer*, 74–75.

115. Welcome, *Fred Archer*, 40.

116. "Spirit of the Times," *Spirit of the Times* 5 November 1887, 508.

117. Christopher McGrath, *Mr. Darley's Arabian* (New York: Pegasus, 2017), 196; Welcome, *Fred Archer*, 45–47.

118. McGrath, *Mr. Darley's Arabian*, 204; Welcome, *Fred Archer*, 126–27.

119. McGrath, *Mr. Darley's Arabian*, 203–4.

120. "Horse Gossip," *Turf, Field and Farm* 26 November 1886, 470; McGrath, *Mr. Darley's Arabian*, 203–4; Welcome, *Fred Archer*, 156.

121. Welcome, *Fred Archer*, 158.

122. "Horse Gossip," *Turf, Field and Farm* 26 November 1886, 470; *Spirit of the Times* 27 November 1886, 560; *New York Sportsman* 27 November 1886, 457.

123. "Horse Gossip," *Turf, Field and Gossip* 10 December 1886, 510.

CHAPTER 3. "I Ride to Win"

1. David W. Blight, *Frederick Douglass: Prophet of Freedom* (New York: Simon & Schuster, 2018), 682–83.

2. "Isaac Murphy," *Lexington Leader* 20 March 1889, 3.

3. Nancy O'Malley, "The Pursuit of Freedom: The Evolution of Kinkead-town, an African American Post-Civil War Neighborhood in Lexington, Kentucky," *Winterthur Portfolio* 37, no. 4 (2002): 209–16.

4. Maryjean Wall, "Kentucky's Isaac Murphy: A Legacy Interrupted, The Intersection of Race and the Horse Industry," MA thesis, University of Kentucky, 2003, 97.

5. W. Fitzhugh Brundage, "Working in the 'Kingdom of Culture': African Americans and American Popular Culture, 1890–1930," *Beyond Blackface: African Americans and the Creation of American Popular Culture, 1890–1930,* ed. W. Fitzhugh Brundage (Chapel Hill: University of North Carolina Press, 2011), 9.

6. Deed Book 77, Fayette County Clerk's Office, 528–29.

7. "The Turf," *St. Louis Post Dispatch* 26 February 1888, 6.

8. Deed Book 88, Fayette County Clerk's Office, 300–301; "The McClelland Property Sale," *Lexington Leader* 10 April 1890, 5.

9. "Sport of All Varieties," *Brooklyn Eagle* 16 February 1890, 14.

10. David G. Hackett, "The Prince Hall Masons and the African American Church," *All Men Free and Brethren: Essays on the History of African American Freemasonry,* ed. Peter P. Hinks and Stephen Kantrowitz (Ithaca: Cornell University Press, 2013), 148; Willard B. Gatewood, *Aristocrats of Color: The Black Elite 1880–1920* (Fayetteville: University of Arkansas Press, 2000), 219.

11. George C. Wright, *Racial Violence in Kentucky, 1865–1900* (Baton Rouge: Louisiana State University Press, 1990), 234–37.

12. *Civil Rights Cases,* 109 U.S. 3, 25 (1883).

13. *Proceedings of the Civil Rights Mass-Meeting Held at Lincoln Hall, October 22, 1883* (Washington, DC: C. P. Farrell, 1883), 12, https://omeka.coloredconventions .org/items/show/1194.

14. Anne E. Marshall, *Creating a Confederate Kentucky: The Lost Cause and Civil War Memory in a Border State* (Chapel Hill: University of North Carolina Press, 2010), 99–100.

15. Frederick Douglass, "Address to the National Convention of Colored Men, Louisville, Ky." (Louisville: Courier-Journal Job-Printing, 1883), 5, https:// www.loc.gov/resource/mfd.24003/?.

16. Frederick Douglass, "Self-Made Men," Frederick Douglass Papers, Library of Congress, 6–7, https://www.loc.gov/resource/mfd.29002/?st=gallery.

17. Gregory Bond, "Jim Crow at Play: Race, Manliness, and the Color Line in American Sports, 1876–1916," PhD diss., University of Wisconsin, 2008, 124.

18. James Weldon Johnson, *Along This Way* (New York: Viking, 1933), 208.

19. David K. Wiggins, "Peter Jackson and the Elusive Heavyweight Championship: A Black Athlete's Struggle Against the Late Nineteenth Century Color-Line," *A Question of Manhood,* ed. Darlene Clark Hine and Earnestine Jenkins, vol. 2 (Bloomington: Indiana University Press, 2001), 283–91; David K. Wiggins, *Glory Bound: Black Athletes in a White America* (Syracuse: Syracuse University Press, 1997), 29–30.

20. Louis Moore, *I Fight for a Living: Boxing and the Battle for Black Manhood, 1880–1915* (Urbana: University of Illinois Press, 2017), 37–38.

21. *Cleveland Gazette* 23 August 1890, 2.

22. Kevin K. Gaines, *Uplifting the Race: Black Leadership, Politics, and Culture in the Twentieth Century* (Chapel Hill: University of North Carolina Press, 1996), 4–5, 16–17.

23. "Epistle of Peter," *Oakland Tribune* 17 July 1890, 8.

24. "The Australian Pugilist," *Washington Evening Star* 13 August 1889, 3.

25. "The Pig-Skin Bayard," *Kansas City Star* 13 July 1886, 2.

26. "The Tattler's Tattle," *New York Sportsman* 22 August 1885, 152.

27. Douglas Henry Daniels, *Pioneer Urbanites: A Social and Cultural History of Black San Francisco* (Berkeley: University of California Press, 1990), 107–8.

28. Daniels, *Pioneer Urbanites*, 108.

29. Bond, "Jim Crow at Play," 199–202, 213; Henry Louis Gates, Jr., "Frederick Douglass's Camera Obscura: Representing the Anti-Slave 'Clothed and In Their Own Form,'" *Picturing Frederick Douglass*, ed. John Stauffer, Zoe Trodd, and Celeste-Marie Bernier (New York: Liveright, 2015), 209–11.

30. William Cronon, *Nature's Metropolis: Chicago and the Great West* (New York: W. W. Norton, 1991), 90–92, 281.

31. Julian Ralph, *Our Great West* (New York: Harper and Brothers, 1893), 11–12.

32. Cronon, *Nature's Metropolis*, 9–11.

33. "Lucky Baldwin's Ranch," *Chicago Tribune* 8 April 1889, 6; C. B. Glasscock, *Lucky Baldwin* (Indianapolis: Bobbs-Merrill, 1933), 47, 150–51; Hubert Howe Bancroft, *Chronicles of the Builders of the Commonwealth* vol. 3 (San Francisco: History Company, 1892), 334–44.

34. "Remarkable Career of 'Lucky' Baldwin," *Boston Post* 20 March 1902, 6.

35. Population schedules, San Francisco, California, 1880 and 1900 U.S. Census.

36. Quoted in Bancroft, *Chronicles of the Builders*, 369–70; Glasscock, *Lucky Baldwin*, 247–49.

37. Alonzo Phelps, *Contemporary Biography of California's Representative Men* (San Francisco: A. L. Bancroft and Co., 1881), 325–26.

38. Amber Fogle Sergent, "'The Pastime of Millions': James B. Haggin's Elmendorf Farm and the Commercialization of Pedigree Animal Breeding, 1897–1920," PhD diss., University of Kentucky, 2012, 23.

39. Richard White, *"It's Your Misfortune and None of My Own": A New History of the American West* (Norman: University of Oklahoma Press, 1991), 258, 266.

40. Sergent, "'Pastime of Millions,'" 57–61; Richard White, *The Republic for Which It Stands: The United States During Reconstruction and the Gilded Age, 1865–1896* (New York: Oxford University Press, 2017), 612.

41. Michael P. Malone, *The Battle for Butte: Mining and Politics on the Northern*

Frontier, 1864–1906 (Seattle: University of Washington Press, 1981), 40–45; Sergent, "'Pastime of Millions,'" 62.

42. *Prominent and Progressive Americans*, vol. 1 (New York: New York Tribune, 1902), 80; Sergent, "'Pastime of Millions,'" 6, 100–102, 111.

43. "J. B. Haggin, President of Homestake, Is Dead," *Weekly Pioneer Times Mining Review* 24 September 1914, 2; Sven Beckert, *The Monied Metropolis: New York City and the Consolidation of the American Bourgeoisie, 1850–1896* (Cambridge: Cambridge University Press, 1993), 238–65.

44. "List of Members and Rules of the American Jockey Club, 1880," Fairman Rogers Collection, University of Pennsylvania.

45. Peter S. Canellos, *The Great Dissenter* (New York: Simon and Schuster, 2021), 306–7.

46. Heather Cox Richardson, *West from Appomattox: The Reconstruction of America After the Civil War* (New Haven: Yale University Press, 2007), 97–98.

47. White, *Republic for Which It Stands*, 525; Richardson, *West from Appomattox*, 250–52.

48. "The Great Need of Kentucky," *Kentucky Live Stock Record* 23 July 1881, 56.

49. "Negro Emigration from Kentucky," *Kentucky Live Stock Record* 13 March 1880, 169.

50. "Colored Emigration," *Kentucky Live Stock Record* 1 October 1881, 236.

51. *Turf, Field and Farm* 15 June 1883, 410.

52. "Track Talk," *St. Louis Globe Democrat* 6 June 1880, 16.

53. "Turf Notes," *Nashville Daily American* 24 January 1883, 8.

54. "The Colored Archer," *Louisville Courier Journal* 15 May 1890, 2.

55. "Post and Paddock," *Spirit of the Times* 15 December 1883, 592.

56. *Goodwin's Official Annual Turf Guide for 1885* (New York: Goodwin Brothers, 1885), 79.

57. "Latonia," *Spirit of the Times* 13 October 1888, 433.

58. R. Gerald Alvey, *Kentucky Bluegrass Country* (Jackson: University Press of Mississippi, 1992), 139–40.

59. "Post and Paddock," *Spirit of the Times* 18 August 1883, 84.

60. Walter Vosburgh, *Famous American Jockeys* (New York: Saalfield, 1883), 43–44.

61. "Ike, the Black Archer," *St. Louis Post Dispatch* 12 June 1889, 10; "A Jockey's Life," *Chicago Tribune* 10 July 1885, 2; "Jockey Ike Murphy," *Kansas City Star* 11 July 1885, 4.

62. "Ike, the Black Archer," 10.

63. *York Herald* 6 January 1887, 8.

64. "A Rich Jockey," *Milwaukee Weekly Wisconsin* 27 July 1889, 8.

65. "Racing," *New York Sportsman* 21 November 1885, 416.

66. "Turf Notes," *Chicago Inter Ocean* 27 May 1886, 2; "Whip and Spur," *San Francisco Examiner* 4 April 1886, 3.

67. "Personals," *Chicago Tribune* 24 November 1888, 4.

68. "Gleanings," *Birmingham Daily Post* 6 December 1886, 7.

69. "Jockey Murphy's New House," *New York Times* 13 June 1887, 1.

70. "Turf Notes," *Brooklyn Citizen* 19 June 1887, 2; "Notes," *Ottawa Daily Citizen* 17 June 1887, 4.

71. "A Rich Jockey," 8; "Isaac Murphy the Jockey," *Detroit Free Press* 15 July 1889, 1.

72. "New Orleans," *Spirit of the Times* 8 May 1886, 456; "Sports and Sportsmen," *Wilkes-Barre Sunday Leader* 9 May 1886, 21; "Ike, the Black Archer," 10.

73. "Echoes of the Week," *New York Sportsman* 31 August 1889, 194.

74. "The Jockey's Profits," *Fall River Globe* 27 February 1889, 2.

75. "Jockey Murphy Talks," *Philadelphia Times* 27 June 1886, 12.

76. "About Jockeys," *St. Joseph Gazette Herald* 4 November 1888, 7.

77. "Ahead of the Bookies," *St. Louis Post Dispatch* 8 June 1889, 28.

78. John H. Davis, *The American Turf* (New York: John H. Polhemus, 1907), 102–3.

79. "Chats with the Horsemen," *St. Louis Globe Democrat* 13 June 1886, 6.

80. "Some Fast Horseflesh," *Chicago Tribune* 20 June 1887, 3. The scholar Gregory Bond has argued that Black athletes used this language of whiteness in complex ways. See Bond, "Jim Crow at Play," 32.

81. See among multiple reports of this remark, "The Famous Jockey Murphy," *Cleveland Gazette* 20 July 1889, 1.

82. *Topeka Lance* 25 July 1885, 4.

83. "Turf Notes in Brief," *New York Sportsman* 10 August 1889, 129.

84. *Arizona Weekly Journal* 31 July 1889, 2; Bond, "Jim Crow at Play," 48–49.

85. Bond, "Jim Crow at Play," xii–xiii.

86. Bond, "Jim Crow at Play," 228–30.

87. Bond, "Jim Crow at Play," 242; Bryan F. Le Beau, *Currier and Ives: America Imagined* (Washington, DC: Smithsonian Institution, 2001), 308–11.

88. Melanie Hernandez, "Currier & Ives's *Darktown* Series: Recovering White Social Capital Through Violent Satire," *International Journal of Comic Art* 20, no. 2 (2018): 268–78; Bond, "Jim Crow at Play," xiii–xiv, 63–64, 86, 91; Le Beau, *Currier and Ives*, 231–34; Marcy S. Sacks, *Before Harlem: The Black Experience in New York City Before World War I* (Philadelphia: University of Pennsylvania Press, 2006), 55–56.

89. Marcy S. Sacks, "Creating Black New York at Century's End," *Slavery in New York*, ed. Ira Berlin and Leslie M. Harris (New York: New Press, 2005), 332–35; Sacks, *Before Harlem*, 44–56.

90. "Racing Notes," *Turf, Field and Farm* 27 September 1889, 343; "St. Louis," *Spirit of the Times* 25 June 1887, 729; "Colored Jockeys Show the Way," *New York Herald* 20 September 1889, 8.

91. "His Trick Didn't Win," *Memphis Avalanche* 3 August 1888, 8; "Echoes of the Day," *New York Sportsman* 21 January 1888, 57; "Turf Notes in Brief," *New York Sportsman* 26 October 1889, 395; "Winning Jockeys," *Turf, Field and Farm* 20 September 1889, 321.

92. "Saratoga," *Spirit of the Times* 18 August 1888, 124.

93. "The Talk of New York," *Brooklyn Eagle* 21 October 1888, 2.

94. Anthony Hamilton passport application, 5 June 1903, U.S. Passport Applications, 1895–1925, Accessed Ancestry.com; Lyman Horace Weeks, *The American Turf* (New York: Historical Company, 1898), 395; "Echoes of the Day," *New York Sportsman* 5 February 1887, 122.

95. "American Jockeys," *Buffalo Enquirer* 24 July 1891, 3; "Some Famous Jocks," *St. Louis Post Dispatch* 14 July 1892, 3; "Five Famous Jockeys," *St. Louis Post Dispatch* 28 November 1889, 3.

96. "A Wealthy Negro Horse Jockey," *Milwaukee Sentinel* 6 January 1884, 9; "Gotham Gossip," *Nashville Daily American* 30 December 1883, 11.

97. "Murphy the Jockey," *Kentucky Live Stock Record* 1 September 1888, 136; "Personals," *Kentucky Live Stock Record* 1 September 1888, 137; *New York Sportsman* 27 July 1889, 75; "Turf Gossip," *Kentucky Live Stock Record* 16 March 1889, 167.

98. "Brooklyn Jockey Club, Gravesend, N.Y.," *Kentucky Live Stock Record* 8 September 1888, 148–49; "Gossip from J.K.S.," *Lexington Leader* 17 March 1889, 4; "Saratoga Association," *Kentucky Live Stock Record* 3 August 1889, 69; "Coney Island Jockey Club, Sheepshead Bay N.Y.," *Kentucky Live Stock Record* 7 September 1889, 149; "Brooklyn Jockey Club, Gravesend, N.Y.," *Kentucky Live Stock Record* 28 September 1889, 195–97; "New York Jockey Club," *Kentucky Live Stock Record* 12 October 1889, 228–29.

99. "Fitzpatrick's Fine Finish," *New York Herald* 23 May 1889, 5; "Kentucky Association Races," *Turf, Field and Farm* 11 May 1888, 407; "Brooklyn Jockey Club Races," *Turf, Field and Farm* 18 May 1888, 429.

100. "Lorillard Day at Monmouth," *New York Herald* 9 July 1889, 8; "Washington Park Club, Chicago, Ill.," *Kentucky Live Stock Record* 22 September 1888, 181–83.

101. "New Orleans," *Spirit of the Times* 1 March 1890, 228; "Post and Paddock," *Spirit of the Times* 3 May 1890, 649.

102. *Spirit of the Times* 5 November 1887, 508–9.

103. "Turf Notes," *San Francisco Examiner* 7 November 1887, 4; "Will Retire," *Lexington Leader* 18 June 1888, 4; "Jockeys Cannot Fight Against Nature," *New Orleans Picayune* 19 September 1888, 3.

104. "Turf Notes," *San Francisco Examiner* 5 December 1887, 4.

105. "Saratoga," *Spirit of the Times* 3 September 1887, 185.

106. *New York Sportsman* 3 September 1887, 225; "Racing," *New York Sportsman* 17 September 1887, 266.

107. "Turf and Training Notes," *New York Sportsman* 1 October 1887, 313; "Horse Gossip," *Turf, Field and Farm* 30 September 1887, 278.

108. "Live Stock and Turf," *Louisville Courier Journal* 14 May 1888, 8.

109. Leon W. Taylor, "Isaac Murphy Winner of Fourteen American Derbies," *Abbott's Monthly* July 1932, 47.

110. "Winner of Two Oaks," *Louisville Courier Journal* 17 May 1889, 2.

111. "'Brown Dick' Owner of Ben Brush," *Thoroughbred Record* 18 May 1895, 310; Walter S. Vosburgh, *Racing in America, 1866–1921* (New York: Jockey Club, 1922), 166–67; "Racing Notes," *Turf, Field and Farm* 27 September 1895, 431; "Ben Brush by His Moustache," *Thoroughbred Record* 9 May 1896, 219.

112. Kent Hollingsworth, "A Man Who Knew Champions," *Blood-Horse* 24 November 1975, 5153.

113. "Horses in Training," *Turf, Field and Farm* 31 March 1888, 194.

114. "Lexington, Ky.," *Spirit of the Times* 24 December 1887, 733; "Racing," *New York Sportsman* 16 February 1889, 151.

115. "Colors Claimed," *New York Sportsman* 28 April 1888, 396; "Lexington Turf Notes," *New York Sportsman* 28 April 1888, 397; "Isaac Murphy, the Colored Jockey," *Buffalo Sunday Morning News* 6 May 1888, 6.

116. "The Sporting World," *Nashville Daily American* 16 July 1888, 3.

117. *Goodwin's Official Annual Turf Guide for 1888* (New York: Goodwin Brothers, 1888), 92–100; "Fine Sport at Lexington," *New York Herald* 10 May 1888, 5; "Brooklyn Jockey Club Races," *Turf, Field and Farm* 18 May 1888, 429.

118. *Goodwin's Guide 1888*, 129, 132, 167, 174, 228; "Turf Notes," *St. Louis Globe Democrat* 15 July 1888, 11; "Chicago," *Spirit of the Times* 21 July 1888, 941–42.

119. "Turf Nomenclature," *New York Sportsman* 28 August 1886, 193; "Sporting News," *Butte Miner* 25 October 1886, 4; "Saddle and Sulky," *Chicago Inter Ocean* 22 April 1888, 19; "Here's Your Horses," *Kentucky Live Stock Record* 14 April 1889, 5.

120. "The Third Day," *Louisville Courier Journal* 13 August 1886, 2; "Echoes of the Week," *New York Sportsman* 8 September 1888, 223.

121. "Isaac Murphy's Position as a Jockey," *Kentucky Live Stock Record* 25 February 1888, 113.

122. "Turf Topics," *Kansas City Times* 2 March 1890, 2; "Among the Thoroughbreds," *St. Louis Post Dispatch* 9 February 1890, 16; "Stars of the Pigskin," *St. Louis Post Dispatch* 6 April 1890, 25.

123. "Exciting Events at Lexington," *Kansas City Times* 10 May 1890, 2.

124. "Kentucky Derby Gossip," *Cincinnati Enquirer* 12 May 1890, 2.

125. "The Kentucky Derby," *Louisville Courier Journal* 20 April 1890, 6.

126. "How the Derby Was Won," *Lexington Leader* 16 May 1890, 1; "Run in the Mud," *San Francisco Call* 15 May 1890, 1.

127. "May Ride Riley Again," *Memphis Daily Commercial* 19 May 1890, 5; "Racing Notes," *Turf, Field and Farm* 23 May 1890, 608.

128. "Haggin Signs Isaac Murphy," *San Francisco Call* 11 May 1890, 1; "Sporting Notes," *Chicago Inter Ocean* 15 May 1890, 2.

129. Osborn House card with address and notation of board, Isaac Murphy Collection, Keeneland Library; "Nearby Resorts," *Brooklyn Standard Union* 25 June 1898, 2.

130. "The Big Suburban," *St. Louis Post Dispatch* 17 June 1890, 2.

131. "A Suburban for Salvator," *New York Times* 18 June 1890, 1–2.

132. "Salvator Wins," *New York World* 18 June 1890, 1–3.

133. "The Futurity," *Spirit of the Times* 8 September 1888, 252; "Purchase of Prince Charlie for America," *Turf, Field and Farm* 10 August 1883, 101.

134. Francis Trevelyan, "Some Points About the Physiognomy of Race Horses That Plainly Indicate Their Disposition," *San Francisco Examiner* 29 December 1900, 8.

135. *Goodwin's Official Annual Turf Guide for 1889* (New York: Goodwin Brothers, 1890), 248, 262–63, 292, 463, 552, 561; Vosburgh, *Racing in America,* 147.

136. Weeks, *American Turf,* 117.

137. "Racing Notes," *Turf, Field and Farm* 20 June 1890, 719.

138. "Salvator Wins," 1–3; "A Splendid Turf Triumph," *Brooklyn Eagle* 18 June 1890, 4.

139. "Salvator By a Neck," *Baltimore Sun* 18 June 1890, 1; "What the Jockeys Said About the Suburban," *Turf, Field and Farm* 20 June 1890, 719.

140. "Tenny's Owner's Opinion," *Turf, Field and Farm* 20 June 1890, 719; "Racing Notes," *Turf, Field and Farm* 27 June 1890, 745.

141. "Tenny-Salvator Match," *Cincinnati Enquirer* 23 June 1890, 2.

142. "Tenny or Salvator—Which?," *San Francisco Examiner* 24 June 1890, 1.

143. "Salvator By a Neck," *St. Paul Globe* 26 June 1890, 5.

144. "Post and Paddock," *Spirit of the Times* 28 June 1890, 1014.

145. "Salvator Wins," *Atlanta Constitution* 29 June 1890, 5.

146. "Salvator By a Neck," *St. Paul Globe,* 5.

147. *Goodwin's Official Annual Turf Guide for 1890* (New York: Goodwin Brothers, 1891), 277; "Racing Notes," *Turf, Field and Farm* 4 July 1890, 14.

148. "Instantaneous Photography," *Wilson's Photographic Magazine* 15 November 1890, 699–700.

149. "Earnest Contests Draw," *Turf, Field and Farm* 4 July 1890, 7.

150. "Opinions on Great Horses," *Thoroughbred Record* 16 August 1924, 75.

151. *Goodwin's Guide 1890*, 346.

152. "The Equine Champions," *Brooklyn Times Union* 13 August 1890, 4; "Salvator the King," *Philadelphia Inquirer* 13 August 1890, 2; "Poor Tenny," *Brooklyn Eagle* 13 August 1890, 2.

153. "Salvator the Champion," *Brooklyn Eagle* 13 August 1890, 12; "The Equine Champions," 4; "Monmouth Park, Long Branch, N.J.," *Kentucky Live Stock Record* 16 August 1890, 99–100.

154. "Salvator Is King," *Brooklyn Eagle*, 13 August 1890, 2.

155. "Post and Paddock," *Spirit of the Times* 16 August 1890, 142–43.

156. "Post and Paddock," *Spirit of the Times* 30 August 1890, 226; "The Drugged Jockey," *Washington Evening Star* 28 August 1890, 7; "Salvator's Worshippers," *New York Sun* 25 August 1890, 6.

157. Shawn Leigh Alexander, *An Army of Lions: The Civil Rights Struggle Before the NAACP* (Philadelphia: University of Pennsylvania Press, 2012), 5.

158. Alexander, *Army of Lions*, 7–11; Emma Lou Thornbrough, *T. Thomas Fortune: Militant Journalist* (Chicago: University of Chicago Press, 1972), 107.

159. Alexander, *Army of Lions*, 12–17.

160. Alexander, *Army of Lions*, 25–33.

161. Carla L. Peterson, *Black Gotham: A Family History of African Americans in Nineteenth-Century New York City* (New Haven: Yale University Press, 2011), 372–73; Thornbrough, *T. Thomas Fortune*, 100.

162. Alexander, *Army of Lions*, 39–40, 52–53; Peterson, *Black Gotham*, 373–74; Thornbrough, *T. Thomas Fortune*, 117–19.

163. T. Thomas Fortune, "The Race Problem: The Negro Will Solve It," *Belford's Magazine* 5, no. 28 (September 1890), 489; Alexander, *An Army of Lions*, 21–22.

164. Fortune, "The Race Problem," 490–91.

165. "The League Convention," *New York Age* 25 January 1890, 1.

166. "Sports and Sportsmen," *New York Age* 18 April 1891, 4; "The World and the Church," *Indianapolis Freeman* 19 July 1890, 7.

167. "Sports and Sportsmen," 4.

168. T. Thomas Fortune, "The Prince of Jockeys," *New York Age* 5 July 1890, 1.

CHAPTER 4. "The Wrong This Day Done"

1. "Post and Paddock," *Spirit of the Times* 7 June 1890, 878.

2. Kent Hollingsworth, *The Great Ones* (Lexington: Blood-Horse, 1970), 113.

3. *Goodwin's Official Annual Turf Guide for 1889* (New York: Goodwin Brothers, 1890), 201, 205, 255, 260, 294, 344, 351, 390, 396–37, 460, 558; *Goodwin's Official Annual Turf Guide for 1890* (New York: Goodwin Brothers, 1891), 279, 282, 445, 449.

4. Hollingsworth, *Great Ones,* 113.

5. "Coney Island Jockey Club, Sheepshead Bay, L.I.," *Kentucky Live Stock Record* 28 June 1890, 403–4; "Monmouth Park, Long Branch, N.J.," *Kentucky Live Stock Record* 9 August 1890, 82–83.

6. *Goodwin's Guide 1890,* 501.

7. "A Monmouth Sensation," *New York Times* 27 August 1890, 3; "Fell from His Saddle," *Chicago Tribune* 27 August 1890, 6.

8. Lyman Horace Weeks, *The American Turf* (New York: Historical Company, 1898), 134.

9. *Buffalo Morning Express* 30 August 1890, 4.

10. "Milk Punches," *Brooklyn Times Union* 28 August 1890, 2; "More About Milk Punches," *Brooklyn Times Union* 29 August 1890, 2; "Apollinaris Natural Mineral Water," *Turf, Field and Farm* 15 February 1878, 107; "Apollinaris Natural Mineral Water," *Kentucky Live Stock Record* 24 November 1877, 336.

11. "Post and Paddock," *Spirit of the Times* 30 August 1890, 226; "Isaac Murphy's Statement," *Brooklyn Citizen* 28 August 1890, 3; "Jockey Murphy Guilty," *New York World* 28 August 1890, 1; "Murphy's Strange Illness," *New York Tribune* 28 August 1890, 7; "Jockey Murphy Pleads Vertigo," *New York Herald* 28 August 1890, 8; "Isaac Murphy Suspended," *New York Sun* 29 August 1890, 5; "Murphy Suspended," *Lexington Leader* 29 August 1890, 1.

12. "Turf and Training Notes," *New York Sportsman* 27 August 1887, 204; "El Rio-Rey Tomorrow," *St. Louis Post Dispatch* 12 June 1889, 9.

13. "Gossip of the Day," *Louisville Courier Journal* 27 April 1888, 8; "A Jockey's Life," *Chicago Tribune* 10 July 1885, 2; Henry Vizetelly, *A History of Champagne with Notes on the Other Sparkling Wines of France* (New York: Scribner and Welford, 1882), 259–60.

14. Christopher Poole, "Cauthen's Agony No Real Surprise," *London Standard* 13 December 1985, 47.

15. Henry Stull, "Thoroughbreds of the Golden State," *Spirit of the Times and Sportsman* 15 June 1895, 770; "1:35½, Salvator, King of the Runners!," *Spirit of the Times* 6 September 1890, 262; "Post and Paddock," *Spirit of the Times* 6 September 1890, 266; "He Is King," *Brooklyn Eagle* 29 August 1890, 4.

16. *Goodwin's Guide 1890*, 505, 537, 541.

17. "Isaac Murphy's Mistake," *New York Sun* 27 August 1890, 5.

18. "King of the Turf," *Sacramento Union* 29 August 1890, 1.

19. "Murphy Disgraced," *Brooklyn Citizen* 27 August 1890, 3.

20. "Jockey Murphy Drugged or Drunk," *New York Herald* 27 August 1890, 8.

21. "A Monmouth Sensation," 3.

22. "Fistiana," *Oakland Tribune* 3 July 1890, 5; "Wealth for Negroes," *Kansas City Times* 8 May 1892, 11.

23. Edward O. Frantz, *The Door of Hope: Republican Presidents and the First Southern Strategy* (Gainesville: University Press of Florida, 2011), 62.

24. *Buffalo Morning Express* 30 August 1890, 4.

25. "Raceland's Manhattan," *New York World* 2 October 1890, 6; "Post and Paddock," *Spirit of the Times* 4 October 1890, 436–37.

26. "Was Isaac Murphy Poisoned," *Chicago Inter Ocean* 17 November 1890, 2.

27. "Isaac Murphy's Condition," *Butte Daily Post* 30 December 1890, 1; "Murphy Sick," *Lexington Leader* 10 October 1890, 1; "Isaac Murphy's Condition," *Chicago Tribune* 23 November 1890, 7; "Race and Stake," *Louisville Courier Journal* 29 December 1890, 6; "Tales of the Turf," *Honolulu Daily Bulletin* 27 March 1891, 1.

28. "The Kentucky Association," *Kentucky Live Stock Record* 9 May 1891, 290–91.

29. "KINGMAN," *Louisville Courier Journal* 14 May 1891, 7.

30. "The Derby Winner," *St. Paul Globe* 18 May 1891, 8.

31. *Goodwin's Guide 1890*, 200, 244, 293, 295, 360.

32. "The Kentucky Association," *Kentucky Live Stock Record* 16 May 1891, 306–8.

33. "The Derby Candidates," *Nashville Daily American* 9 May 1891, 2.

34. "Racing Notes," *Turf, Field and Farm* 22 May 1891, 629.

35. "KINGMAN," 6.

36. "The Kentucky Derby," *Baltimore Sun* 14 May 1891, 3.

37. "Louisville Jockey Club," *Kentucky Live Stock Record* 16 May 1891, 308; "Post and Paddock," *Spirit of the Times* 16 May 1891, 755; "Louisville," *Spirit of the Times* 23 May 1891, 785–86.

38. "Sport at Morris Park," *Chicago Tribune* 31 May 1891, 17.

39. "Jockey Hamilton to Be Married," *New York Times* 12 January 1891, 1; "Jockey Hamilton Married," *New York Times* 23 January 1891, 5.

40. "Murphy Entertains," *Lexington Leader* 25 January 1891, 5; "Grand Reception Given by Isaac Murphy and Wife, to Anthony Hamilton and Bride," *Lexington Transcript* 25 January 1891, 5.

41. "Colored Social Events," *Lexington Leader* 10 June 1891, 2.

42. "Britton-Jackson, The Noted Colored Jockey, Thos. Britton, Is United," *Lexington Transcript* 6 May 1891, 1.

43. "Colored Society," *Lexington Leader* 17 April 1892, 5.

44. "Won Fame as a Jockey," *Lexington Leader* 31 January 1893, 2.

45. "Colored Contributors," *Lexington Leader* 15 January 1893, 6.

46. "Cinderella," *Lexington Leader* 26 May 1895, 7.

47. "The Great Colored Fair," *Indianapolis Freeman* 3 October 1891, 3; W. D. Johnson, *Biographical Sketches of Prominent Negro Men and Women of Kentucky* (Lexington: Standard, 1897), 79–84.

48. Anne E. Marshall, "Kentucky's Separate Coach Law and African American Response, 1892–1900," *Register of the Kentucky Historical Society* 98, no. 3 (2000): 241–46.

49. Marshall, "Kentucky's Separate Coach Law," 247; Patricia Hagler Minter, "The Codification of Jim Crow: The Origins of Segregated Railroad Transit in the South, 1865–1910," PhD diss., University of Virginia, 1994, 141–42.

50. Rev. S. E. Smith, ed., *History of the Anti-Separate Coach Movement of Kentucky* (Evansville: National Afro-American Journal and Directory Publishing, 1895), 15.

51. "A Woman's Appeal to Members of the Kentucky General Assembly," *Lexington Leader* 19 April 1892, 3.

52. Johnson, *Biographical Sketches,* 18.

53. Smith, *History of the Anti-Separate Coach Movement,* 58, 61, 154–55; Johnson, *Biographical Sketches,* 65–66.

54. Marshall, "Kentucky's Separate Coach Law," 249–51.

55. Marshall, "Kentucky's Separate Coach Law," 251.

56. Smith, *History of the Anti-Separate Coach Movement,* 51.

57. Marshall, "Kentucky's Separate Coach Law," 253–55.

58. "Clay," *Cincinnati Enquirer* 13 June 1894, 2; "Ejected from a Smoking Car," *Louisville Courier Journal* 13 June 1894, 1; "Will Sue the L&N," *Lexington Leader* 14 June 1894, 8.

59. "Tenny's Marvelous Run," *Chicago Tribune* 31 June 1891, 6; "Monmouth Park Association," *Kentucky Live Stock Record* 15 August 1891, 98.

60. "Rey Del Rey's Good Chances," *Chicago Tribune* 27 August 1890, 6.

61. "To Wed a Title," *Chicago Inter Ocean* 6 July 1890, 8.

62. "Mr. Ehret Buys Out Mr. Winters," *Turf, Field and Farm* 29 August 1890, 249.

63. "McLewee to be Sued by Jockey McLaughlin," *St. Louis Globe Democrat* 10 June 1891, 4.

64. "Racing Notes," *Turf, Field and Farm* 19 June 1891, 740.

65. "The Turf," *New York World* 29 July 1891, 1; "New York Jockey Club," *Kentucky Live Stock Record* 20 June 1891, 387; "Monmouth Park Association," *Kentucky Live Stock Record* 18 July 1891, 35; "Monmouth Park Association," *Kentucky Live Stock Record* 8 August 1891, 81; "Coney Island Jockey Club, Sheepshead Bay, L.I.," *Kentucky Live Stock Record* 12 September 1891, 162–63; "Brooklyn Jockey Club," *Kentucky Live Stock Record* 26 September 1891, 193–95; "New York Jockey Club," *Kentucky Live Stock Record* 17 October 1891, 226–27; "Brooklyn Jockey Club," *Kentucky Live Stock Record* 28 May 1892, 410–11; "New York Jockey Club," *Kentucky Live Stock Record* 17 June 1892, 474–75; "Racing at Long Branch," *Turf, Field and Farm* 15 July 1892, 74.

66. "The Turf," *New York World* 4 August 1892, 5; "Ike Murphy in Trouble with His Stable," *Chicago Tribune* 27 July 1892, 7; "Post and Paddock," *Spirit of the Times and Sportsman* 30 July 1892, 49.

67. "Isaac Murphy Sues for His Salary," *Buffalo Enquirer* 24 October 1892, 3.

68. Richard Rovere, *Howe & Hummel: Their True and Scandalous History* (Syracuse: Syracuse University Press, 1996), 6–9, 107–12, 124–25.

69. Rovere, *Howe & Hummel*, 14–15, 25–26, 125–26.

70. Rovere, *Howe & Hummel*, 19–20, 77, 102–3.

71. "Post and Paddock," *Spirit of the Times and Sportsman* 29 October 1892, 538–39; Weeks, *American Turf*, 51.

72. "Tips from the Turf," *Lexington Leader* 20 November 1893, 8.

73. "Out at Churchill Downs," *Kentucky Live Stock Record* 18 February 1893, 109; "Sporting Notes," *Chicago Inter Ocean* 8 September 1892, 7.

74. "In the Bluegrass," *Louisville Courier Journal* 13 March 1892, 9.

75. "Talk of the Turf," *New York World* 15 November 1892, 1.

76. "Horsemen and Horses," *Chicago Inter Ocean* 19 April 1891, 6; *Goodwin's Annual Official Turf Guide for 1891* (New York: Goodwin Brothers, 1892), 282, 292, 653, 689; "Isaac Murphy Buys the Hero," *Lexington Leader* 13 January 1892, 1.

77. "Turf Notes," *Chicago Tribune* 24 January 1892, 7; "At the Running Track," *Lexington Leader* 13 March 1892, 3; "Track Talk," *St. Louis Post Dispatch* 27 July 1892, 8.

78. "Valiant's Fast Work," *Lexington Leader* 2 April 1894, 6; "Out at the Kentucky Association Course," *Kentucky Live Stock Record* 17 March 1894, 161; "Madge," *Cincinnati Enquirer* 9 April 1894, 2; "A Good Day," *Lexington Leader* 31 May 1894, 8.

79. Walter S. Vosburgh, *Racing in America, 1866–1921* (New York: Jockey Club, 1922), 44; Dan M. Bowmar, *Giants of the Turf* (Lexington: Blood-Horse, 1960), 115–16.

80. "To Trainers and Jockeys," *Spirit of the Times and Sportsman* 31 March 1894, 370.

81. Kent Hollingsworth, *The Kentucky Thoroughbred* (Lexington: University Press of Kentucky, 1976), 117–18; Maryjean Wall, *How Kentucky Became Southern* (Lexington: University Press of Kentucky, 2010), 190–92.

82. "The Licensing of Jockeys," *Spirit of the Times and Sportsman* 3 March 1893, 251.

83. "Jockey Club Rules," *Chicago Tribune* 4 May 1894, 11.

84. Foxhall Keene, *Full Tilt: The Sporting Memories of Foxhall Keene* (New York: Derrydale, 1938), 33–34.

85. "At Churchill Downs," *Louisville Courier Journal* 16 February 1891, 5.

86. "How Simms Was Discovered," *Thoroughbred Record* 9 February 1895, 87.

87. "Local Turf News," *Kentucky Live Stock Record* 12 January 1895, 23.

88. "Ike Thompson's Views," *New York Sun* 5 May 1895, 8; "The Spirit of the Times," *Spirit of the Times and Sportsman* 27 April 1895, 520.

89. "Southern Racing," *Spirit of the Times and Sportsman* 28 January 1893, 46; "Western Racing," *Spirit of the Times and Sportsman* 15 June 1895, 772; Weeks, *American Turf,* 386, 394.

90. Steve Thomas, "Link to 1895," *Blood-Horse* 19 April 1986, 2812–13.

91. "It Was Perkins Day," *Lexington Transcript* 21 October 1893, 1; "A Short Sketch of Jockey Perkins," *Lexington Transcript* 22 October 1893, 5; "Western Light-Weight Jockeys," *Kentucky Live Stock Record* 25 August 1894, 117.

92. "Local Turf News," *Kentucky Live Stock Record* 4 November 1893, 296.

93. "Local Turf News," *Kentucky Live Stock Record* 5 January 1895, 6.

94. "Nashville," *Spirit of the Times* 9 May 1891, 701.

95. "Racing Notes," *Spirit of the Times* 21 February 1891, 193.

96. Gregory Bond, "Jim Crow at Play: Race, Manliness, and the Color Line in American Sports," PhD diss., University of Wisconsin, 2008, 268; "Horse Gossip," *Turf, Field and Farm* 25 September 1891, 362.

97. "The Vanity Among Jockeys," *Thoroughbred Record* 17 November 1894, 317.

98. "A Popular Meeting," *Spirit of the Times and Sportsman* 19 October 1895, 455.

99. "Nashville," *Spirit of the Times and Sportsman* 7 May 1892, 639–40; "Ephraim Grizzard Lynched by White Mob in Nashville, Tennessee," https://calendar.eji.org/racial-injustice/apr/30.

100. "Taral Won the Handicap," *New York Tribune* 5 June 1896, 3.

101. "Amusements," *Nebraska State Journal* 5 October 1894, 6.

102. "The Derby Winner," *St. Louis Post Dispatch* 26 May 1894, 33; "New Plays Seen," *Brooklyn Standard Union* 26 February 1895, 3.

103. "Western Racing," *Spirit of the Times and Sportsman* 1 December 1894, 670.

104. "The Derby Winner," *Lexington Leader* 27 November 1894, 4; "The Derby Winner," *Lexington Leader* 30 December 1894, 7.

105. "Racing at Latonia," *Kentucky Live Stock Record* 2 June 1894, 337; "Say He Was Drunk," *Chicago Inter Ocean* 29 May 1894, 5.

106. "New Orleans," *Spirit of the Times and Sportsman* 22 February 1896, 156.

107. Isaac Murphy Will, 30 January 1893, Will Book 8, Fayette County Clerk's Office, 160.

108. "Local Turf News," *Thoroughbred Record* 16 March 1895, 170.

109. "Turf Topics," *Lexington Leader* 28 March 1895, 6; "City and Vicinity," *Lexington Leader* 18 April 1895, 2.

110. "Sporting," *Nashville American* 19 May 1895, 6.

111. "Hamilton Surprised," *Philadelphia Times* 17 June 1895, 8; "Murphy Disappointed," *Philadelphia Times* 17 June 1895, 8; "Lazzarone Vindicated," *Thoroughbred Record* 22 June 1895, 392.

112. "Erratic Rey El Santa Anita," *New York Sun* 23 August 1895, 4; "Rey El Santa Anita Doped," *San Francisco Call* 24 August 1895, 2.

113. *Goodwin's Annual Official Turf Guide for 1895* vol. 2 (New York: Goodwin Brothers, 1896), ccxlvii.

114. "Isaac Murphy's Death," *Thoroughbred Record* 15 February 1896, 79.

115. *Nottnagel & Bro. v. Isaac Murphy,* Case #4261; *W. T. Jones v. Isaac Murphy,* Case #2213; *Louis and Gus Straus v. Isaac Murphy,* Case #2215, Fayette County Circuit Court Records, Kentucky Department of Libraries and Archives.

116. Indenture between Isaac Murphy and Lucy B. Murphy and Gust. Luigart, 12 July 1894, Deed Book 103, Fayette County Clerk's Office, 348–49; Indenture between Isaac B. Murphy and Lucy B. Murphy and Magdalen D. Davidson, 7 December 1895, Deed Book 107, Fayette County Clerk's Office, 261.

117. "Grand Opening at the English Kitchen," *Lexington Leader* 6 June 1891, 7.

118. *Williams' Lexington City Directory for 1881–2* (Williams and Co., 1881), 122; "Luigart's Opening," *Lexington Leader* 24 December 1890, 2.

119. Mortgage Book 43, Fayette County Clerk's Office, 267–69.

120. "Isaac Murphy, The Noted Jockey and Horse-Owner, Dies Last Night," *Lexington Herald* 12 February 1896, 8.

121. Isaac Murphy, death certificate, 12 February 1896, Accessed Ancestry.com.

122. "Funeral of Isaac Murphy," *Lexington Herald* 14 February 1896, 5; "Noted Jockeys To Act as Pall Bearers at Isaac Murphy's Funeral," *Lexington Leader* 14 February 1896, 8; "LAST RITES," *Lexington Leader* 16 February 1896, 1; "Among the Tombs," *Lexington Herald* 17 February 1896, 1; "Laid to Rest," *Lexington Leader* 17 February 1896, 5; "Isaac Murphy: Lincoln Lodge of Masons Adopts Resolutions on His Death," *Lexington Leader* 16 March 1896, 7.

123. *Plessy v. Ferguson,* 163 U.S. 537, 555, 559, 562 (1896).

CHAPTER 5. Afterlives

1. "A Lawn Fete," *Lexington Leader* 9 September 1897, 6.

2. "Isaac Murphy's Estate," *Buffalo Evening News* 24 February 1896, 4.

3. *George Luigart v. Lucy B. Murphy,* Case #3370, Fayette County Circuit Court Records, Kentucky Department of Libraries and Archives.

4. "Lexington Canning Co.," *Lexington Leader* 8 November 1898, 2; "It Is Sold," *Lexington Leader* 15 February 1898, 1; "Delay," *Lexington Leader* 7 August 1898, 8; *Luigart v. Murphy,* Fayette County Circuit Court Records.

5. *Luigart v. Murphy,* Fayette County Circuit Court Records; Deed Book 119, Fayette County Clerk's Office, 328–29; "Commissioner's Sale," *Lexington Leader* 11 February 1900, 11.

6. "Die Poor," *Lexington Leader* 12 February 1898, 7.

7. "Brown Dick Passes Away," *Louisville Courier Journal* 12 May 1906, 7.

8. Pamela Lyons Brinegar first made this comparison.

9. Lucy Murphy death certificate, 26 February 1910, Accessed Ancestry .com; "Isaac Murphy's Widow Dead," *Louisville Courier Journal* 26 February 1910, 11.

10. "Colored News," *Lexington Leader* 27 February 1910, Sec. 2, 15.

11. Susie Osborn death certificate, 8 April 1919, Accessed Ancestry.com; "Colored Notes," *Lexington Leader* 10 April 1919, 5; Settlement Book 16, Fayette County Clerk's Office, 518–20.

12. *Who's Who of the Colored Race* vol. 1, ed. Frank Lincoln Mather (Chicago: 1915), 43; "Attempt at Segregation Leads to Suit," *Pittsburgh Courier* 28 June 1924, 2; "Journalist," *Pittsburgh Courier* 17 March 1928, 8; "Memory of Turf King Recalled as Classic Kentucky Derby Looms," *Pittsburgh Courier* 18 May 1929, 16.

13. "Large Attendance at the Negro Fair," *Lexington Leader* 12 September 1906, 2.

14. "Bluegrass Turf Gossip," *New Orleans Times-Democrat* 4 July 1904, 10; "Colored," *Lexington Leader* 12 December 1905, 2; "Fayette Instructs for A. E. Wilson," *Lexington Leader* 15 June 1907, 1; "Colored Taft Clubs," *Lexington Leader* 2 April 1912, 7.

15. "A Gala Day," *Lexington Leader* 3 January 1899, 1–2.

16. Abraham Murphy Perry, World War I draft registration card, Accessed Ancestry.com; *Polk's Lexington City Directory 1928* (Columbus, OH: R. L. Polk and Co., 1928), 426.

17. A. J. Liebling, *Just Enough Liebling* (New York: North Point Press, 2004), 270.

18. Steven A. Riess, *Horse Racing the Chicago Way: Gambling, Politics, and Organized Crime* (Syracuse: Syracuse University Press, 2022), 265; Liebling, *Just Enough Liebling,* 270.

19. William H. P. Robertson, *The History of Thoroughbred Racing in America* (Englewood Cliffs, NJ: Prentice Hall, 1964), 196–97, 213, 316; Maryjean Wall, *How Kentucky Became Southern* (Lexington: University Press of Kentucky, 2010), 228–32.

20. "Winkfield Tells How Alan-a-Dale Won," *Louisville Courier Journal* 4 May 1902, Sec. 3, 2; "Booker Thinks His Ride Won the Race," *Louisville Courier Journal* 3 May 1903, Sec. 3, 3; "Jockey Winkfield Did Well in Russia This Year," *Louisville Courier Journal* 11 December 1904, Sec. 3, 6; Roy Terrell, "Around the World in Eighty Years," *Sports Illustrated* 8 May 1961, 71–88.

21. "Black Star Shines," *Louisville Times* 6 June 1907, 16.

22. *Goodwin's Annual Official Turf Guide for 1907* vol. 2 (New York: Goodwin Brothers, 1908), ccxii.

23. "Jockey J. Lee," *Thoroughbred Record* 8 June 1907, 370.

24. "Rides Six Winners," *Indianapolis Freeman* 15 June 1907, 7.

25. "The Abbot Wins the Latonia Derby in Mud," *Louisville Courier Journal* 11 June 1907, 9.

26. "Gossip of the Racetrack," *New York Sun* 23 May 1908, 5.

27. "Local Turf News," *Thoroughbred Record* 25 February 1899, 90; "Jockey War at Chicago," *Thoroughbred Record* 18 August 1900, 77; "Racing at Washington Park," *Turf, Field and Farm* 27 June 1902, 617; "Jockeys Draw Line on Color," *Atlanta Constitution* 5 November 1904, 9; "Passing of Negro as Rider," *Oklahoma News* 18 December 1906, 3; "Few Negro Jockeys Left," *Washington Post* 11 January 1907, 8; "In the World of Sport," *Indianapolis Freeman* 26 January 1907, 7; "What Has Become of Negro Jockeys?," *Monroe News-Star* 8 June 1929, 9.

28. Debra Barbezat and James Hughes, "Finding the Lost Jockeys," *Historical Methods* 47, no. 1 (2014): 20–26; Michael Leeds and Hugh Rockoff, "Jim Crow in the Saddle: The Expulsion of African American Jockeys from American Racing," Working Paper 28167, NBER Working Paper Series, December 2020. Copy in possession of author.

29. *St. Louis Republic* 10 January 1904, Sec. 3, 7.

30. "Negro Jockeys Shut Out," *New York Times* 29 July 1900, 14.

31. "In the World of Sports," *Indianapolis Freeman* 11 November 1905, 6.

32. Hugh Keough, "Passing of the Colored Jockeys," *Louisville Courier Journal* 14 January 1902, 6.

33. "The Thoroughbred," *Turf, Field and Farm* 18 August 1899, 844; "Attempt Failed," *Lexington Leader* 12 August 1899, 7.

34. "Took His Own Life," *Lexington Leader* 20 May 1901, 7; "Lost $50 on a Race," *Lexington Leader* 20 May 1901, 7.

35. "'Soup' Perkins Last Noted Negro Rider," *Lexington Leader* 12 September 1911, 10; "Colored Notes," *Lexington Leader* 21 August 1911, 7.

36. "Training Jockeys," *Thoroughbred Record* 24 October 1896, 201; "On the Turf," *San Francisco Chronicle* 2 August 1896, 10; "Pool Rooms Threaten Life of Horse Racing," *Nashville Banner* 15 June 1907, 11.

37. "Is the Black Jockey Doomed," *Topeka Plaindealer* 27 July 1906, 1.

38. "Negro Riders of Renown," *Daily Racing Form* 17 February 1922, 1.

39. "Day of Colored Jockey—Can Any One Explain—Seems to Have Passed," *National Police Gazette* 11 April 1903, 3.

40. "Drawing the Color Line," *Wilkes-Barre Record* 9 January 1909, 19.

41. "Stake-winning Jockeys of This Year," *Daily Racing Form* 30 December 1908, 3.

42. James Baldwin, *The Fire Next Time* (New York: Vintage, 1993), 5–6.

43. Anne E. Marshall, *Creating a Confederate Kentucky: The Lost Cause and Civil War Memory* (Chapel Hill: University of North Carolina Press, 2010), 166–70; Anne E. Marshall, "The 1906 *Uncle Tom's Cabin* Law and the Politics of Race and Memory in Early-Twentieth-Century Kentucky," *Journal of the Civil War Era* 1, no. 3 (2011): 384–87; "To See 'Birth of a Nation,'" *Lexington Leader* 26 February 1916, 4; Gregory A. Waller, *Main Street Amusements: Movies and Commercial Entertainment in a Southern City, 1896–1930* (Washington, DC: Smithsonian Institution, 1995), 101–2, 153–58, 177.

44. "Famous American Jockeys," *Thoroughbred Record* 6 March 1920, 180–81.

45. "An Old-Timer's Memories Turn Back to Westport's Fairground of the '80s," *Kansas City Times* 21 June 1945, 18.

46. "Field of Twenty May Go to Post," *Louisville Courier Journal* 19 May 1928, 1.

47. Sheena C. Howard and Ronald L. Jackson, II, eds., *Black Comics: Politics of Race and Representation* (London: Bloomsbury, 2013), 105; Ponchitta Pierce, "What's Not So Funny About the Funnies," *Ebony* November 1966, 52–55.

48. "Johnson and Jeffries Championship Battle," *Indianapolis Freeman* 2 July 1910, 7.

49. Jack Johnson, *My Life and Battles,* ed. and trans. Christopher Rivers (Westport, CT: Praeger, 2007), 16–17; Geoffrey C. Ward, *Unforgiveable Blackness: The Rise and Fall of Jack Johnson* (New York: Alfred A. Knopf, 2004), 13.

50. Leon W. Taylor, "Isaac Murphy Winner of Fourteen American Derbies," *Abbott's Monthly* July 1932, 47.

51. James Weldon Johnson, *Black Manhattan* (New York: Alfred A. Knopf, 1930), 76.

52. "Isaac Murphy in Diorama," *The Negro Star* 17 May 1940, 1.

53. Paul Devlin, ed., *Rifftide: The Life and Opinions of Papa Joe Jones as Told to Albert Murray* (Minneapolis: University of Minnesota Press, 2011), 79–80.

54. Taylor, "Isaac Murphy Winner of Fourteen American Derbies," 47.

55. Frank B. Borries, Jr., "Ike Murphy, Famed Negro Jockey, Buried in Lexington—Not in Alabama," *Lexington Leader* 5 May 1961, 13.

56. Borries, "Ike Murphy, Famed Negro Jockey, Buried in Lexington—Not in Alabama," 13.

57. Frank Borries, "Ike Murphy's Grave," *Louisville Courier Journal Magazine* 7 May 1961, 16.

58. "Worner Revisited," *New Yorker* 13 April 1981, 32–33.

59. Isaac Murphy Material, Box 2, Keeneland Library; Frank B. Borries, Jr., "Ike Murphy—Now Forgotten—Was a Racing Record Maker," *Lexington Leader* 15 January 1967, D10–11.

60. "Dedication Isaac Burns Murphy Memorial Man o' War Park," Isaac Murphy Material, Box 1, Death, Funeral, Grave, Reburial Folder, Keeneland Library; "Isaac Murphy Monument to Be Dedicated May 4," *Lexington Leader* 30 April 1967, 16.

61. Earl Ruby, "Bet the Jockey and Win? Only on One—Ike Murphy," *Louisville Courier Journal* 5 May 1967, B4.

62. "Suit Filed Challenging Right to Punish Cassius," *Lexington Leader* 30 April 1967, 16.

63. Mel Heimer, "New Resting Place Found for King of 1800 Jockeys," *Poughkeepsie Journal* 7 May 1967, 16C.

64. David J. Garrow, *Bearing the Cross: Martin Luther King and the Southern Christian Leadership Conference* (New York: William Morrow, 1986), 560–61; Luther Adams, *Way Up North in Louisville: African American Migration in the Urban South, 1930–1970* (Chapel Hill: University of North Carolina Press, 2010), 174–77; Tracy E. K'Meyer, *Civil Rights in the Gateway to the South: Louisville, Kentucky, 1945–1980* (Lexington: University Press of Kentucky, 2009), 129–31, 142–43.

65. K'Meyer, *Civil Rights in the Gateway to the South,* 129–30.

66. "Five Youths Dash in Front of Horses During Race," *Louisville Courier Journal* 3 May 1967, B1.

67. "Isaac Murphy Gets New Resting Place," *Louisville Defender* 4 May 1967, 1; "Demonstrators 'Prep' for Derby Effort; Carmichael Due Here," *Louisville Defender* 4 May 1967, 1; "Derby Demonstrations Neither Helpful nor Prudent," *Louisville Defender* 4 May 1967, 6.

68. "Housing March Downtown, Not at Downs," *Louisville Courier Journal* 7 May 1967, A1; Adams, *Way Up North in Louisville,* 178–80; K'Meyer, *Civil Rights in the Gateway to the South,* 135–36.

69. K'Meyer, *Civil Rights in the Gateway to the South,* 135–36; Kent Hollingsworth, "A Misty 93rd Kentucky Derby," *Blood-Horse* 13 May 1967, 1208.

70. Adams, *Way Up North in Louisville,* 181; K'Meyer, *Civil Rights in the Gateway to the South,* 136–42.

71. "Kid Glove Handling of Mobs Won't Work," *Lexington Herald* 4 May 1967, 4.

72. "Disturbed," letter to the editor, *Lexington Herald* 7 May 1967, 4.

73. John Alexander, "Isaac Murphy Now Legend to Thoroughbred Racing," *Lexington Leader* 4 May 1967, 11.

74. David Alexander, "Delayed Honors," *Thoroughbred Record* 6 May 1967, 1176.

75. W. B. Ardery, "Murphy's Bones," *Lexington Leader* 7 May 1974, 15; John Alexander, "Body of Jockey Who Won 3 Derbies May Not Go to Park," *Lexington Leader* 7 May 1974, 5.

76. Bob Considine, "Champion's Rest for Ike Murphy," *Lexington Leader* 7 May 1967, 5.

77. Will Grimsley, "Gravesites Changes," *Central New Jersey Home News* 4 May 1977, 20.

78. Amy Wilson, "Groom's Son Remembers Life Growing up Around Man O' War," *Lexington Herald-Leader* 2 October 2010.

79. Sandra McKee, "Rich History in Recovery," *Baltimore Sun* 14 May 1997, D1.

80. William Doyle, interview by Joseph McMillan, 21 March 1995, African Americans and the Backside Interviews, Kentucky Oral History Commission, Kentucky Historical Society.

81. Larry Bonafon, interview by Joseph McMillan, 24 March 1995, African Americans and the Backside Interviews, Kentucky Oral History Commission, Kentucky Historical Society.

82. Kent Hollingsworth, "A Man Who Knew Champions," *Blood-Horse* 24 November 1975, 5154–56.

83. Maryjean Wall, "In Their Own Words," *Lexington Herald-Leader* 26 August 2001, K2.

84. Wall, "In Their Own Words," K1.

85. Milton C. Toby, "No Blinking Lights Needed," *Blood-Horse* 13 June 1977, 2456; Dan Mearns, "Off the Gold Standard," *Blood-Horse* 27 June 1977, 2461; Art Grace, "A Challenge Met," *Blood-Horse* 6 February 1978, 594–95.

86. "Oscar Dishman, Jr., Thoroughbred Horse Trainer for More Than 40 Years, Dies at 77," *Lexington Herald-Leader* 3 October 2000; Oscar Dishman, Jr., interview, 16 September 1986, Blacks in Lexington Oral History Project, Louie B. Nunn Center for Oral History, University of Kentucky Libraries.

87. Rick Cushing, "In Recent Years, Derby Hasn't Been Mixed Race," *Louisville Courier Journal* 30 April 1990, D3.

88. Dave Mesrey, "The Iron Man of Hazel Park: Wayne Barnett's Improbable Comeback," *Detroit Metro Times* 1 October 2016.

89. Jennifer Hewlett, "Park to Honor African-American Horse Racing Legacy," *Lexington Herald-Leader* 7 December 2006, A-1; Merlene Davis, "Bring Your Shovel to the Isaac Murphy Art Garden," *Lexington Herald-Leader* 10 May 2011.

90. Joe Drape, "Pull Out of the Kentucky Derby? Pressure on a Black Owner Mounts," *New York Times* 3 September 2020; Tim Sullivan, "The Only Black Owner in the Kentucky Derby Wants to Use the Event as a Platform, not a Protest," *Louisville Courier Journal* 4 September 2020; Alaa Elassar, "Activists Want an African American Horse Owner to Boycott the Kentucky Derby," CNN 5 September 2020, https://www.cnn.com/2020/09/05/us/kentucky-derby-louisville-breonna-taylor-greg-harbut-trnd/index.html.

91. Drape, "Pull Out of the Kentucky Derby?"; Jerry Dixon, Sr., interview with Real Players Inside the Backstretch, 9 May 2022, https://www.youtube.com/watch?v=6ZcE6GXqNk8.

92. Najja Thompson, "Commentary: The Horse Racing Industry Must Increase Racial Diversity," *Albany Times Union* 21 March 2021; Jordan Strickler, "Society Offers Minorities Leg Up in Horse Racing Industry," University of Kentucky College of Agriculture, Food and Environment News 3 February 2022, https://news.ca.uky.edu/article/society-offers-minorities-leg-horse-racing-industry.

93. Teresa Genaro, "Jockey Carmouche Hopes for Progress on Race Issues," *Bloodhorse* 8 June 2020, https://www.bloodhorse.com/horse-racing/articles/241648/jockey-carmouche-hopes-for-progress-on-race-issues.

94. Howard Amos, interview with Joseph McMillan, 29 November 1994, African Americans and the Backside Interviews, Kentucky Oral History Commission, Kentucky Historical Society.

ACKNOWLEDGMENTS

THIS BOOK EXISTS because of the expertise and generosity of Becky Ryder, Roda Ferraro, Kelly Coffman, Katie Farmer, and Dan Prater. Every researcher should be lucky enough to work at the Keeneland Library. The Fayette County Clerk's office heroically provided me with a huge pile of crucial documents in the midst of a pandemic, and Irma Johnson of Kentucky State University graciously helped me visit and navigate the KSU collections. I would also like to thank the staffs at the University of Kentucky Library, the Kentucky Historical Society, the Lexington Public Library's Kentucky Room, the Kentucky Department of Libraries and Archives, and the Woodford County Historical Society.

The best part of working on this project has been the friends I have made in central Kentucky. I am immensely thankful for Ed Bowen's friendship and unerring writer's eye, which have enriched both my life and this book. Yvonne Giles has unearthed and preserved the stories of the Black horsemen of the Lexington track, and we should all be thankful to her. Yvonne kindly shared her research with me and inspired me to continue. She also introduced me to Pam Brinegar, whose archival discoveries and insight into America and Lucy Murphy's lives are integral to this project. When COVID and teaching made travel impossible for me, Abigail Stephens and Emily Libecap provided invaluable research assistance. The folks at Phoenix Rising in Lexington are working hard to celebrate and continue the legacies of Black horsemen, and Bill Cooke and the staff at the International Museum of the Horse are doing the same online, with the Chronicle of African Americans in the Horse Industry. I am proud to support their work. Researching this subject has brought me into contact with the descendants of generations of African American horsemen, and I thank them profoundly for sharing their families' pasts with me.

In Lexington, Marsha and Walter Bloxsom welcomed me into their home, for which I cannot thank them enough. Bill and Jan Marshall were unfailingly kind and supportive. I know I am only one of the many people who will miss Bill. Liz Westin has been my friend since I first started coming to Kentucky to do research more than a decade ago; may that continue always.

I could not have completed this project without the support and the friendship of Jim Jones. I hope he knows all that he has done to enrich my life. Ed Gray read this manuscript with acuity and grace and did more than his part to help me feel welcome at FSU. Paul Renfro, Will Hanley, Laurie Wood, George Williamson, and Joe Gabriel are the best book support group there could be. Pam Robbins and Randy Smookler are the best salon partners. Claudia Liebeskind, Ben Dodds, Cathy McClive, Maxine Jones, Meghan Martinez, Jenna Pope, and Devin Burns teamed up to keep me at least moderately sane, and I deeply appreciate it and them. Kathryn Olivarius, Joe Geylin, and Beryl all helped me write this book, but that's only one of the many reasons they are dear to me. Margaret Johnson, Ryan Brasseaux, Jan Bradshaw, and Lincoln Mayer helped sustain me when things got hard. I'm so glad Margaret and I can still laugh together when we're working on deadline. Months into the pandemic, with archives closed for the foreseeable future, Monica Westin showed me how I could complete research absolutely necessary to this book; with a few minutes of cheerful, determined insight, she saved this project, and her friendship is a gift. Kim and Karen Townsend went through every stage of this manuscript with me and offered expert analysis in both horses and prose. They are the best of friends.

My thanks also go to the series editors and the staff at Yale University Press. Amanda Gerstenfeld fielded my questions and worries with aplomb. Noreen O'Connor-Abel and Joyce Ippolito were ideal editors: thoughtful, kind, and meticulous. Everyone at the River Ridge branch of PJ's deserves acknowledgment for caffeinating this book. Maranatha Stables welcomed me and gave me back something I thought I'd never have again. My family and my students, as always, have given me infinite gifts.

INDEX

———

.